CW01659391

THE ART OF HOKUS

MASTERPIECES OF JAPANESE P

THE CHESTER BEATTY LIB

About the author

Dr Clare Pollard has a degree in Japanese Studies from Cambridge University and a doctorate on the subject of 19th-century Japanese ceramics from Oxford University. She has spent several years studying in Japan, and has undertaken research at the Kyoto Municipal University of Art, the Tokyo National Museum of Modern Art (Crafts Gallery) and the Tokyo National Museum. She has been Curator of the East Asian Collections at the Chester Beatty Library since 1996.

THE ART OF HOKUSAI

Masterpieces of Japanese Printing in the Chester Beatty Library

Clare Pollard

TOWN HOUSE
DUBLIN

First published in 2003 by
TownHouse, Dublin
THCH Ltd
Trinity House
Charleston Road
Ranelagh
Dublin 6
Ireland

© text, Chester Beatty Library, 2003

© illustrations, The Trustees of the Chester Beatty Library, Dublin, 2003 except © Bibliothèque nationale de France, Paris *Ushigafuchi at Kudan (Kudan Ushigafuchi)* © Victoria & Albert Picture Library, London *Stoneware plate with Manga-inspired design of cockerel* designed by Félix Bracquemond and Eugène Rousseau © National Gallery, London *Les Parapluies* by Pierre-Auguste Renoir © National Museum of Ethnology, Leiden *Self-portrait of Hokusai at the age of eighty-three*

1 2 3 4 5 6 7 8 9 10

All rights reserved. No part of this publication may be reproduced, stored in a retrieval system, or transmitted in any form or by any means, electronic, mechanical, photocopying, recording or otherwise, without the prior permission of the publisher.

A CIP catalogue record for this book is available from the British Library.

ISBN: 1-86059-174-4

Cover and text design by Wendy Williams Design
Typeset by Wendy Williams Design
Printed by Nørhaven Book, Denmark

Contents

For my parents, John and Moyra Pollard

Reading a Japanese Print

SERIES TITLE
富嶽三十六景
ARTIST'S SIGNATURE
前北斎為一筆
PRINT TITLE
下目黒

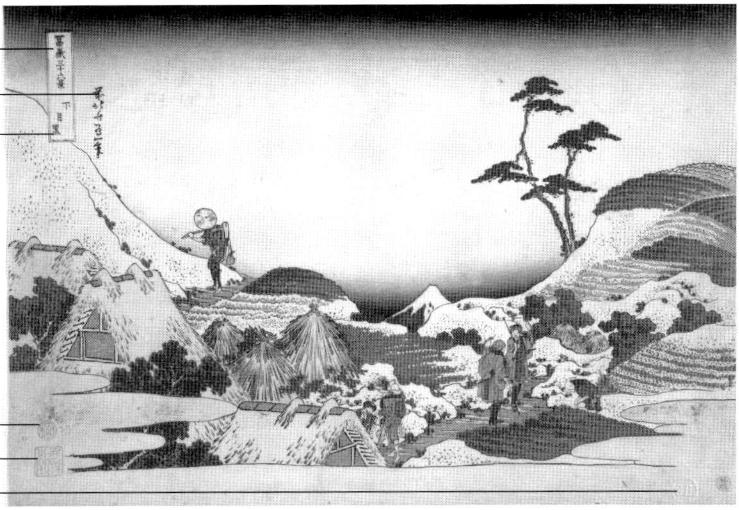

CENSOR'S SEAL
極
PUBLISHER'S SEAL
永寿堂
COLLECTORS' SEALS
林忠正 Chester Beatty

SERIES TITLE	*Fugaku sanjurokkei* (Thirty-Six Views of Mount Fuji)
ARTIST'S SIGNATURE	*zen Hokusai Iitsu hitsu* (drawn by Iitsu, previously known as Hokusai)
PRINT TITLE	*Shimo Meguro* (Lower Meguro)
CENSOR'S SEAL	*Kiwame* (a type of authorisation seal used on woodblock prints published between 1790 and 1842)
PUBLISHER'S SEAL	*Eijudo* (the name of the publishing company belonging to the Edo publisher Nishimuraya Yohachi)
COLLECTORS' SEALS	*Hayashi Tadamasa* (a well-known Japanese art collector and dealer active in the late-19th century) *Chester Beatty*
DATE	1830s

CBL J 2744

A Japanese print may bear several marks and sets of characters.
These will commonly include:
The **title of the print** and – if the print is part of a series – the **title of the series**. This is often framed within a cartouche.
The **artist's signature** and sometimes his official seal which is usually square in shape and often red in colour.
The **censor's seal(s)**. Most prints published between 1790 and 1875 will bear a seal indicating official authorisation. This may be accompanied by another seal giving the date according to the twelve-year Japanese zodiacal calendar cycle.
The **publisher's seal**. The seal of the person who has commissioned the print.
Collectors' seals. Owners of the print may add their own seals.

Katsushika Hokusai: Master of Japanese Printing

The woodblock print designer Katsushika Hokusai (1760–1849) is one of Japan's most celebrated artists. During a hugely productive artistic career that spanned seventy years, he created an astonishing range of works, including pictures of landscapes, beautiful women, actors, birds, flowers and animals, as well as illustrated books, religious images, erotica and brush paintings.

He was undoubtedly the best-known artist in Japan during his lifetime and he was also the first Japanese artist to become popular in the West, where he made an enormous impact on European artists such as Manet, Van Gogh and Toulouse-Lautrec in the late-19th century. He has been the subject of more exhibitions and books than any other Japanese artist, both in Japan and abroad, and his best-known print, *The Great Wave*, has been reproduced in such a variety of designs – from book covers to T-shirts and mouse-mats – that it is familiar to people all over the world.

Hokusai lived during what has been described as the 'golden age' of Japanese woodblock printing. Commercial woodblock printing in Japan developed

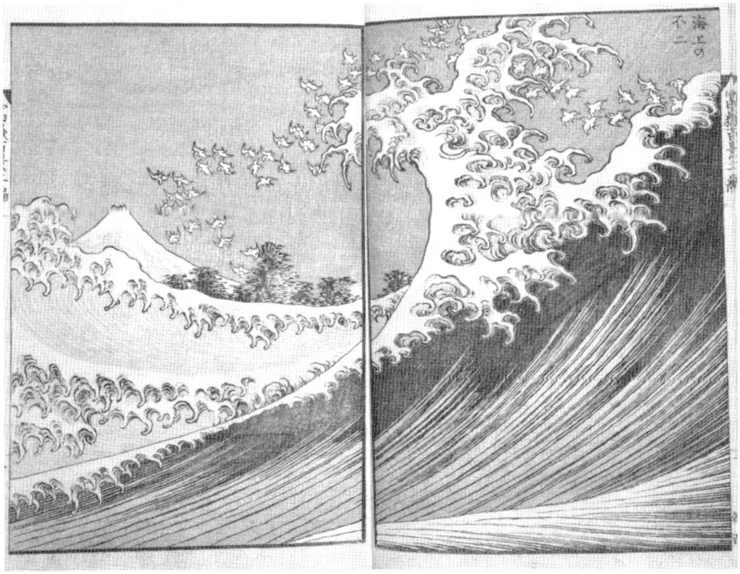

FUJI ABOVE THE WAVES (KAIJO NO FUJI)
From One Hundred Views of Mount Fuji, *vol. 2* (Fugaku hyakkei)
Date: 1835
CBL J 1614

This work, with its dramatic black-and-white designs of Mount Fuji from a variety of different angles, is considered Hokusai's masterpiece of book illustration. Here Mount Fuji is shown beyond a sea of churning waves. What at first glance seem to be large drops of water hurled from the crest of the wave on the right is in fact a flock of sea birds.

rapidly from the 17th century to cater for a growing audience in the major cities. By the late-18th century, it had reached its technical and commercial zenith, with the perfection of full-colour printing techniques and huge numbers of publishers and booksellers producing a wide variety of books and single-sheet prints. The main demand was for *ukiyo-e*, images depicting scenes of fashionable, everyday life in and around the cities. Hokusai is considered one of the outstanding figures of the *ukiyo-e* school of artists. With his superb skills as a draughtsman, accurate powers of observation, sharp sense of humour and broad knowledge of Japanese, Chinese, and Western artistic techniques, Hokusai was a remarkable chronicler of the Japan of his day. Through the medium of the woodblock print, he was able to make his designs available, at a modest price, to unprecedented numbers of people.

Little is known about Hokusai's private life, but he had a reputation for being eccentric and unconventional, with a disregard for personal comfort. Despite his professional success, he never achieved financial security and lived much of his life in relative poverty. He married twice and his children and grandchildren, apart from one faithful daughter who looked after him in his old age, seem to have been a constant source of tribulation. He appears to have lived entirely for his art and is said to have died expressing the wish for just a few more years to perfect his skills.

Sir Alfred Chester Beatty greatly admired Hokusai, whom he considered "one of the most outstanding men in the history of Japanese prints". Beatty's Japanese print collection was formed after his move to Dublin in 1950, when he commissioned Jack Hillier, the eminent English print expert, to put together a representative collection of Japanese woodblock prints and printed books. The foundation of the collection was a large group of prints (including forty-nine works by Hokusai) formerly owned by Dr M Cooper and purchased *in toto* in 1954. Jack Hillier steadily added to this collection over the next decade. Now containing seventy-five single-sheet prints by Hokusai and nine illustrated books, the collection gives a good indication of the extraordinary versatility and energy of this artist – a man who changed his artistic name more than thirty times, his address more than ninety times, left a total oeuvre of some 30,000 designs, and carried on working right up until his death at the age of eighty-nine.

Few details are known about Hokusai's background, but he was born in Edo (present-day Tokyo), the headquarters of the Tokugawa family of *shoguns*, or military rulers. The Tokugawa *shoguns* had unified Japan in 1603 after over a century of civil wars and, until 1867, ruled in the name of the emperor through a network of *samurai* provincial lords. The period of Tokugawa rule was known as the Edo period, after the capital city. Conditions of peace and prosperity during the two-and-a-half centuries of the Tokugawa shogunate led to a flowering of the arts, in particular the popular culture of the merchants, craftsmen and common people in the cities. Although they were of lowly status within the social hierarchy imposed by the *shoguns* and forbidden from any involvement in political activity, these newly wealthy – and often highly educated – commoner classes had plenty of leisure time and money to spend. Excluded from the traditional amusements of the *samurai* and aristocratic classes, they soon developed their own forms of entertainment, which centred around the pleasure districts of the major cities. This frivolous and racy world of brothels, *kabuki* (popular theatre) and teahouses was known as the *ukiyo*, or 'floating world'.

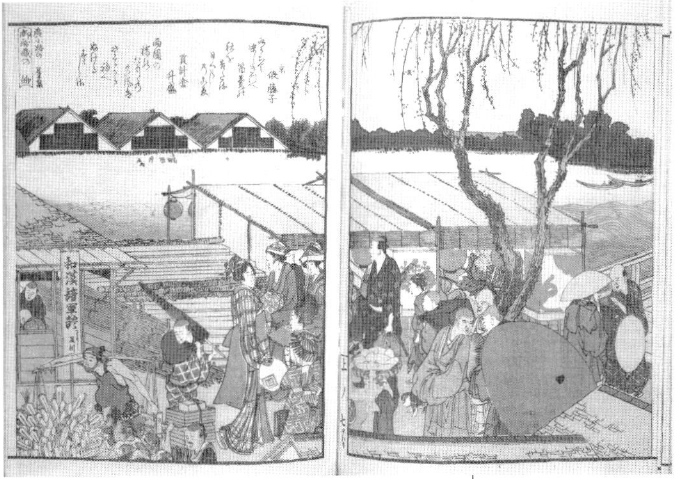

RIVERSIDE STALLS IN EDO
From Both banks of the Sumida River (Ehon Sumidagawa ryogan ichiran)
Date: c.1805
CBL J 1673

This book gives a continuous panoramic view along the banks of the Sumida River, which ran through the city of Edo.

The *ukiyo* generated a whole new body of popular art and literature, featuring heroes with whom the townspeople could identify – not the *samurai* and aristocrats of the classics, but the common people who patronised the pleasure quarters, and the beautiful courtesans and glamorous *kabuki* actors who were its stars. The paintings and woodblock prints depicting these lowlife celebrities were known as *ukiyo-e*, or 'pictures of the floating world'.

Although the term *ukiyo-e* refers to both paintings and prints, today we particularly associate it with the single-sheet woodblock print, a medium that came into its own during the Edo period (1603–1867) and reached its peak just as Hokusai came of age.

While woodblock printing had been practised in Japan from at least as early as the 8th century, until the end of the 16th century it had been used almost exclusively for reproducing Buddhist texts and images. However, with the growth of an increasingly literate, urban audience during the 17th century, non-religious works began to appear – starting with illustrated popular editions of classical tales, but soon developing into new *ukiyo*-related genres. Individual prints of popular *ukiyo* idols began to be produced around 1700 and, for much of the 18th century, were bought chiefly by wealthy merchants. By the time Hokusai was growing up, however, they were available to a much larger audience, with printing being carried out on an almost industrial scale.

Ukiyo-e woodblock prints – whether single-sheet prints or printed books – were mass-produced and their production was organised using a clear division of labour. Prints were produced by a team of highly skilled craftsmen, employed and directed by a publisher. The publisher would commission a design from a print artist, such as Hokusai, who would provide an initial sketch drawn in black ink on paper to the correct dimensions of the woodblock. Once this initial sketch had been approved by a government official, who censored it for licentious content, a professional block-copyist would then work out, on thin paper, a finished drawing for the woodblock, fining down the lines for the engraver. The finished copy was passed to the engraver, who pasted it face down onto a block of seasoned cherry wood, planed along the grain rather than across it in the European manner (which meant that the wood grain was often visible in the background of the print – an effect that could be skilfully used to enhance the design). The block was then carved, using a variety of chisels and gouges, to leave the design standing out in relief in reversed image. Finally, the design was inked and printed up by the printer. The ink was applied to the block and the paper laid onto the block. This differed from Western techniques where the block is applied to the paper. The impression was taken by rubbing the back of the paper with a flat pad called a *baren*.

At first, prints were restricted to black outlines, and were often hand-painted with red and green pigments. In the mid-18th century, however, a registration method was developed that enabled many different colours to be printed on a single sheet of paper. A number of proofs were pulled from the initial 'key block', one for every colour to be used. Separate woodblocks were then carved for each colour, with simple notches called *kento* carved in an identical position at the edges of each block. The sheet of paper used for the print could be aligned against these notches to ensure perfect registration of colour. By Hokusai's day, the art of full-colour printing had been mastered to an astonishing level of finesse and colour prints were cheap enough (costing the equivalent of a bowl of noodles) to be affordable to almost all. *Ukiyo-e* were sold from roadside stalls, shops and teahouses in every city, with Edo – by 1700 already a vast metropolis of a million inhabitants and one of the largest cities in the world – the flourishing centre of *ukiyo-e* production. It is estimated that, during the 19th century, there were over 600 Edo-based print-designers and over 400 publishers active in the field, quite apart from the book-publishing trade, which was mostly separate and much larger.

A BOOKSELLER'S STALL
By Torii Kiyonaga
Date: 1780s
CBL J 2424

In the back left-hand corner of this busy New Year's street scene, the stall of the Edo bookseller Nishimuraya Yohachi (Eijudo) can be seen. Two shop assistants are helping a customer choose a print; the one he holds in his hand shows a courtesan and her assistant.

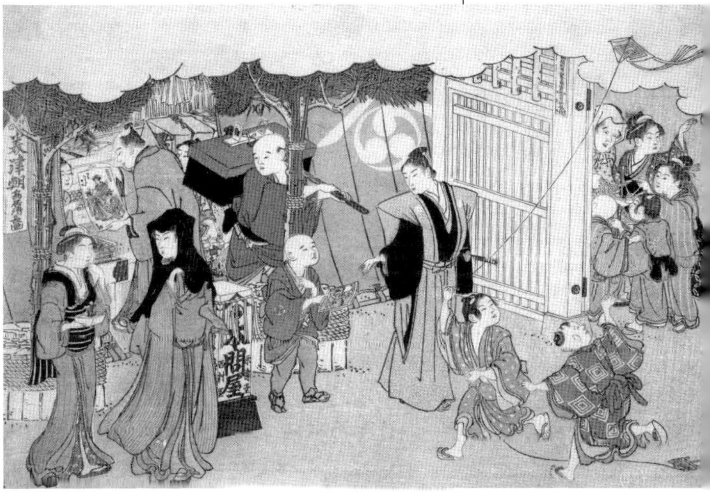

Hokusai, who is said to have been the son of a mirror-maker to the shogunate, became involved with the world of *ukiyo-e* from an early age. After working for a while as an assistant in a bookshop, he spent three years in his mid-teens working as an engraver of wooden printing blocks. This does not mean that he later cut the blocks for his own designs, as it was only in the early-20th century that woodblock print artists, inspired by Western practice, began to cut their own blocks and pull their own prints. However, it is likely that his experience as an engraver gave him an understanding of the technical

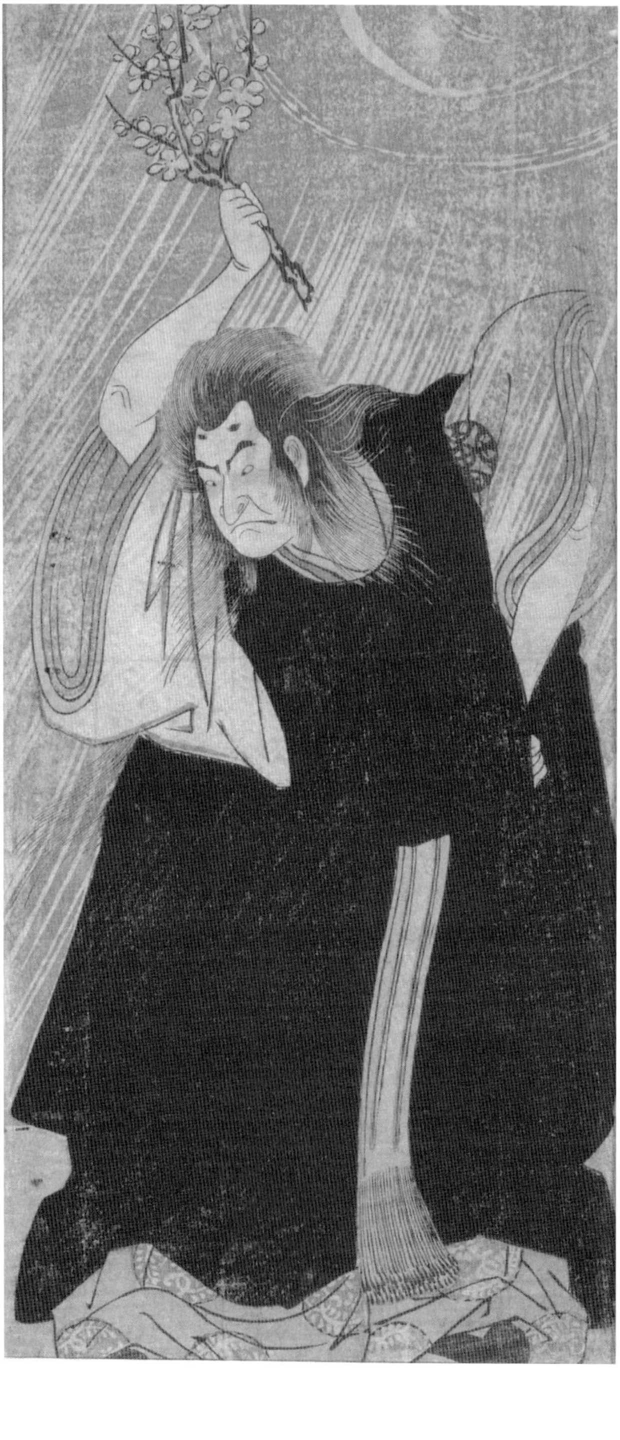

THE ACTOR NAKAMURA NAKAZO I AS THE GHOST OF SUGAWARA MICHIZANE
By Katsukawa Shunsho
Date: c. 1780
CBL J 2608

This print by Hokusai's master, Katsukawa Shunsho, shows a dramatic moment from the final scene of the *kabuki* play *Sugawara Denju*.

skills involved in translating the stylistic nuances of an original ink drawing into the engraved lines of the print block.

Then, at the age of eighteen or nineteen, Hokusai was accepted as a pupil of Katsukawa Shunsho (1726–92), a leading designer of prints of *kabuki* actors. He took the art name of Katsukawa Shunro and his earliest prints were portraits of actors in the style of the Katsukawa School. He also tried his hand at other subjects during this early period of his career, producing designs based on legends and Chinese themes, a number of pictures of beautiful women and *sumo* wrestlers and illustrations for books, chiefly cheap works of popular fiction known as *kibyoshi*.

Surimono: Privately Published Prints

By the mid-1790s, after nearly fifteen years as a pupil of Katsukawa Shunsho, Hokusai broke with the Katsukawa School and its artistic restrictions and began to work in other fields. For a while he studied under Kano Yusen, a master of the classical, Chinese-derived Kano School of painting, but was soon expelled from the studio for criticising his teacher's work. Later he became connected with the Tawaraya School, a group of relatively humble professional painters dedicated to the revival of the Rinpa style of decorative art. However, by the last years of the 18th century, Hokusai struck out on his own and was never again associated with any specific painting school, although he continued to experiment with a wide range of artistic styles throughout his lifetime.

In the meantime, he had begun to make a name for himself as a designer of *surimono* – privately published woodblock prints that were issued to mark special events, such as musical and theatrical performances or poetry recitals. The majority of *surimono* were commissioned by wealthy members of the poetry clubs that became fashionable in the major cities of Japan around the turn of the 18th century. These poetry clubs were composed of art-loving citizens from different classes – merchants, *samurai* and professional artists – brought together by their common love of the arts, and in particular the composition of comic poetry known as *kyoka*. *Kyoka* (literally 'crazy verse')

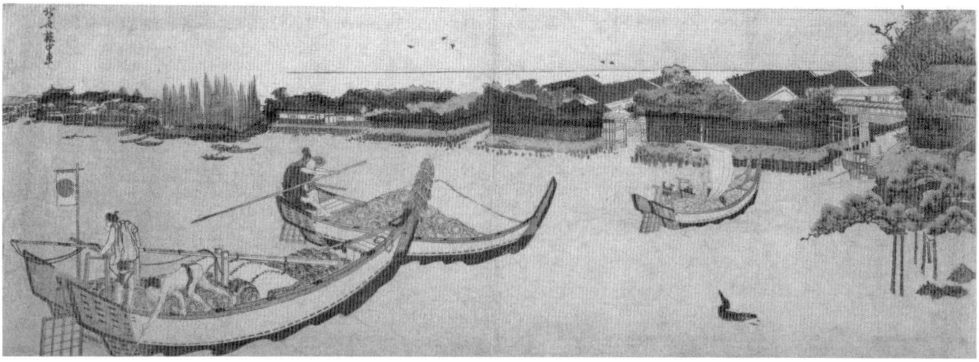

FRONT

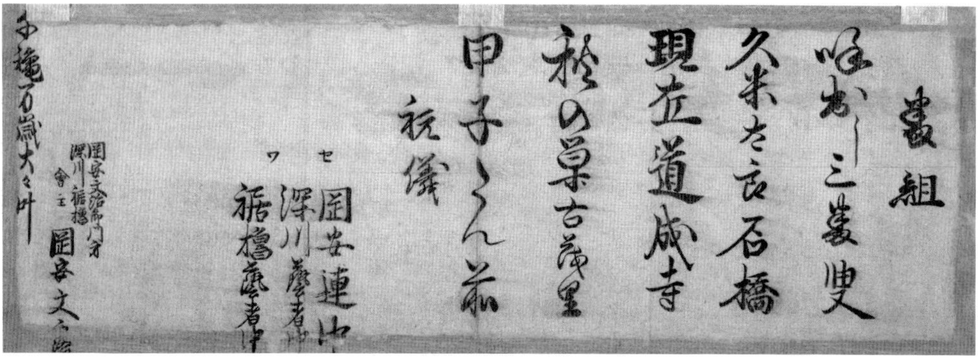

REVERSE

BOATS DELIVERING RICE TO THE GOVERNMENT STOREHOUSES AT ASAKUSA
Signature: Hokusai ryocho ga
Date: 1799 (republished 1804)
CBL J 2795

Four boats laden with bales of rice converge at the entrance to the government rice storehouses on the west bank of the Sumida River. On the back of this *surimono* is pasted the announcement of a programme of *geisha* dances and accompanying chanting, which Hokusai's design was used to illustrate.

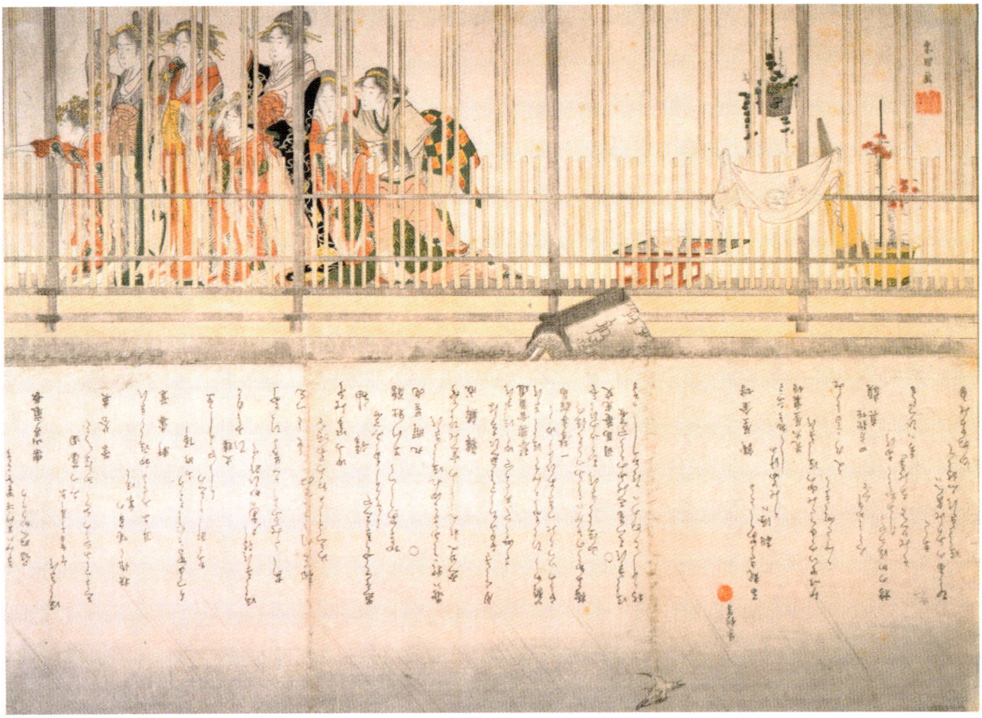

COURTESANS AND ATTENDANTS WATCHING A CUCKOO

Signature: Sori ga, Kyoden sha

Date: late-1870s

CBL J 2819

A group of courtesans from the Daimonjiya brothel stand behind the wooden latticework of their establishment and look out at a cuckoo flying by (the cuckoo is located beneath the text towards the right of the sheet). The print was originally issued folded in six parts, with only the right third of the picture showing. When this flap was opened, the cuckoo appeared outside the window close to the courtesans in the left third of the picture.

There is a poignant contrast between the bird in free flight and the women behind bars. The accompanying poems – three of which are by the courtesans whose portraits appear above – were probably commissioned by the owner of the Daimonjiya or a patron of the establishment.

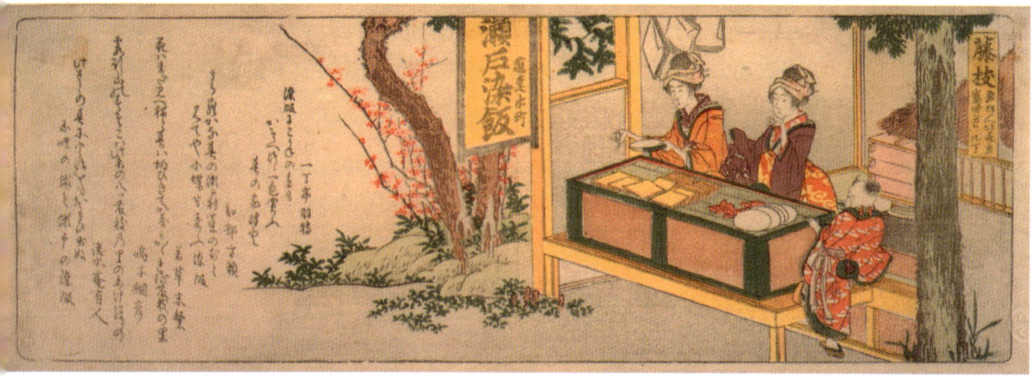

(TOP) **FUJIEDA: TWO RI AND NINE CHO (FIVE-AND-A-HALF MILES) TO SHIMADA**
From an untitled series of stations on the Tokaido Road
Signature: Gakyojin Hokusai ga
Date: 1804
CBL J 2768

The two women are seated at the counter of a shop selling steamed rice cakes to travellers. The cakes were a speciality of Fujieda, one of the stations on the Tokaido Road that linked Edo with the former capital of Kyoto. Made of rice dyed yellow with the sap of the gardenia, the cakes were steamed in the wooden frames seen at the back of the shop. They were sold in flat parcels placed between the stiff white disks that can be seen on the right.

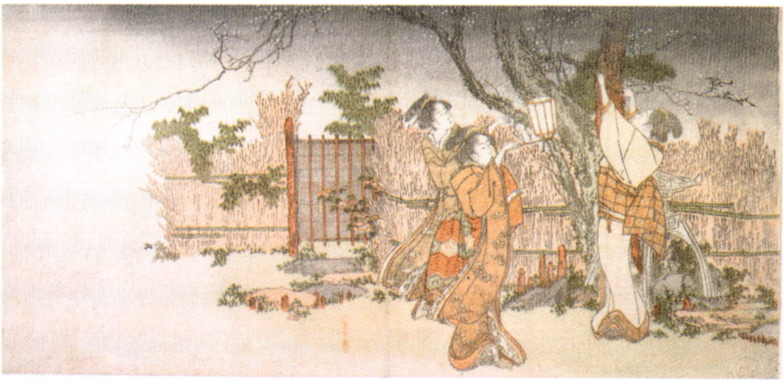

THREE WOMEN BESIDE A PLUM TREE
Unsigned
Date: c.1796
CBL J 2769

In the mid-1790s, Hokusai stopped designing commercial prints and, in 1796, reappeared with a different name, Sori, as a designer of privately commissioned *surimono* and illustrations for albums of *kyoka* comic verse. This picture of a woman breaking a flowering branch from a plum tree has a vertical centrefold and came from one of these albums. Although it is unsigned, the drawing style is characteristic of Hokusai's work around 1796.

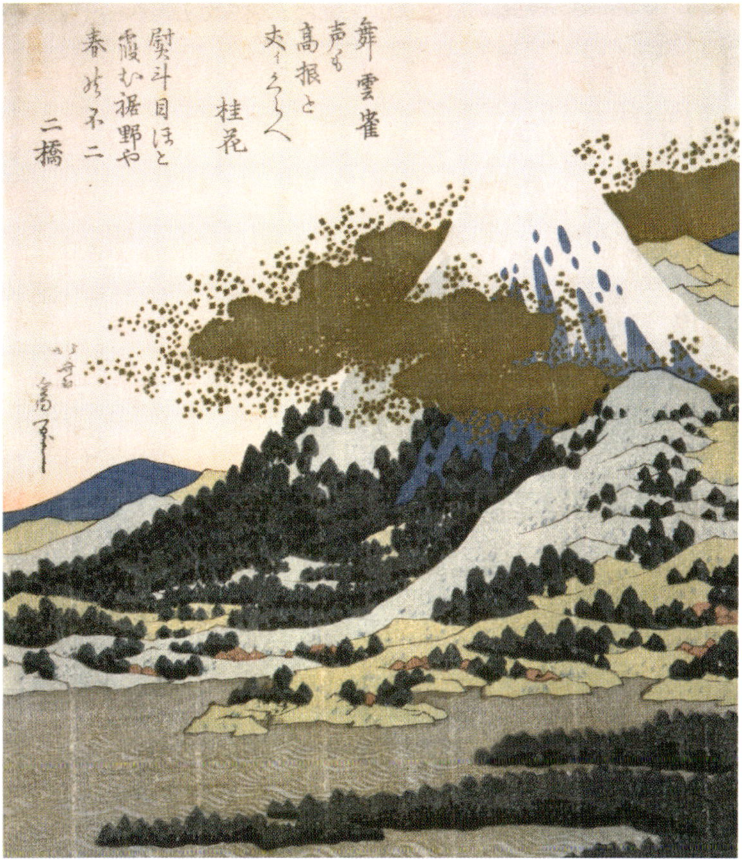

MOUNT FUJI FROM LAKE ASHI IN HAKONE
Signature: Hokusai aratame Iitsu hitsu
Date: early- to mid-1830s
CBL J 2179

It was believed that to dream of Mount Fuji, a hawk or aubergines on the first or second night of the New Year would bring luck in the coming months. For this reason, Mount Fuji often appears on New Year's *surimono*. Hokusai designed very few *surimono* after 1825 but, in the early 1830s, he began to produce his series of 'Thirty-Six Views of Mount Fuji' for a commercial publisher, and it was probably around then that he designed this print.

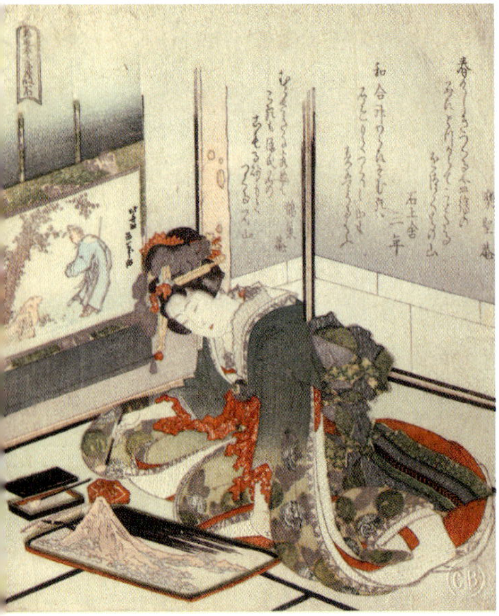

STONE (ISHI)
Series: 'Three pictures for the children's hand game 'scissors, paper, stone'' (Osana asobi ken sanbantsuki no uchi)
Signature: Hokusai aratame Iitsu hitsu
Date: 1823
CBL J 2176

The woman in this exquisitely printed *surimono* is painting the flat surface of a tray landscape, made with a mountain-shaped stone. A painting hangs in the alcove beside her. The subject of the painting is Huang Chuping, a Daoist adept who began his life as a goatherd. Aged fifteen, he found a cave and spent the next forty years there in meditation. When he emerged, he found that his goats had turned into blocks of stone. This not only illustrates the subject of 'stone', but also indicates that the print was published in the spring of 1823, a Goat Year.

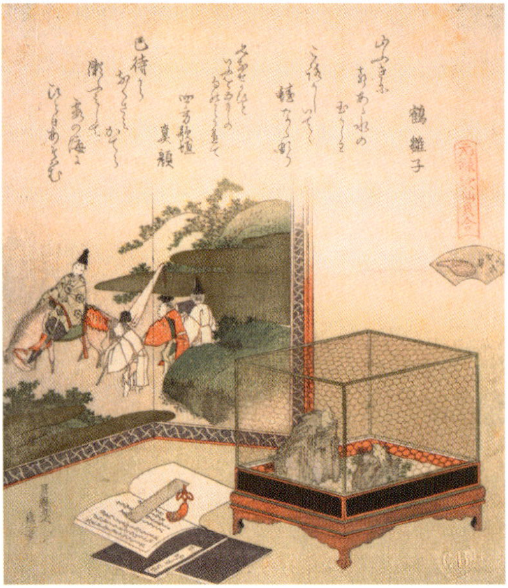

THE MINASE SHELL (MINASEGAI)
Series: 'A Matching Game with the Genroku Poem Shells' (Genroku kasen kai awase)
Signature: Getchirojin Iitsu hitsu
Date: 1821
CBL J 2169

The title of this series of *surimono* refers to a popular pastime in which contestants selected classical poems and matched them to different types of shells. Here, three books and a cage containing rocks and two small frogs stand beside a painted screen. Minase is the name of a river near Kyoto where, in 1488, three famous poets composed a collection of one hundred linked verses entitled 'Three Poets of the Minase River'. Their gathering is symbolised by the three books in the picture. The Minase River was famous for its yellow *yamabuki* flowers, which are illustrated in the screen in the background.

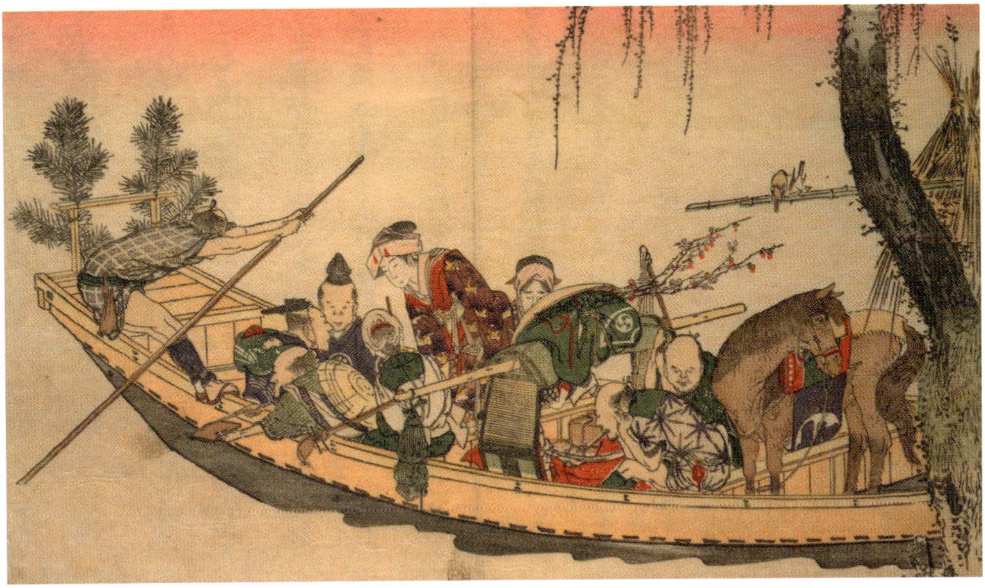

A FERRYBOAT WITH HORSE, PALANQUIN AND TRAVELLERS
From Spring in the Four Directions (Yomo no haru)
Date: 1796
CBL J 1655

This scene of a packed ferryboat at the New Year was Hokusai's contribution to a privately commissioned album of *kyoka* poetry, distributed in the New Year of 1796. Two other artists also contributed illustrations. No expense was spared in the production of this luxury edition, as can be seen by the use of embossing and mica powder.

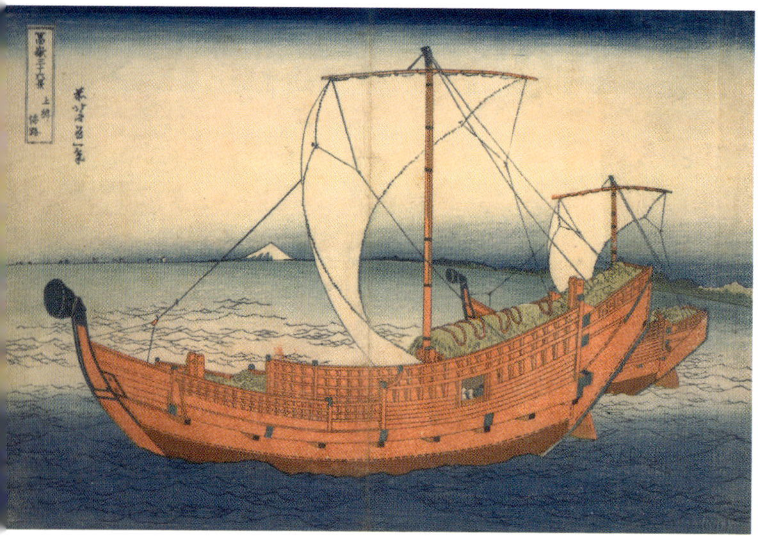

THE SEA OFF KAZUSA (KAZUSA NO KAIRO)
Series: 'Thirty-Six Views of Mount Fuji' (Fugaku sanjurokkei)
Signature: zen Hokusai Iitsu hitsu
Date: mid-1830s
CBL J 2746

A large junk, sailing across the mouth of Tokyo Bay, dominates the scene, with Mount Fuji seen in the distance through its sail rigging. A second junk is partially hidden behind the stern of the first boat. The only sign of life in the picture is the four small figures glimpsed through an open porthole in the nearest junk.

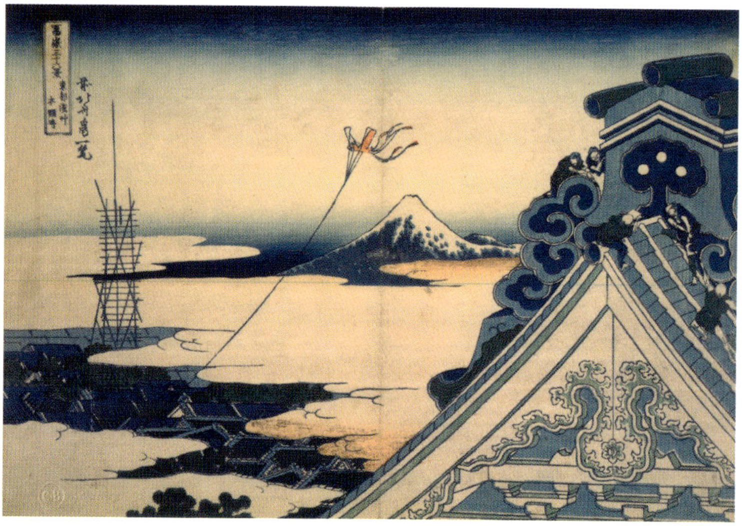

THE HONGANJI TEMPLE AT ASAKUSA IN EDO (TOTO ASAKUSA HONGANJI)
Series: 'Thirty-Six Views of Mount Fuji' (Fugaku sanjurokkei)
Signature: zen Hokusai Iitsu hitsu
Date: c. 1831
CBL J 2749

In this impressive example of Hokusai's love of unusual viewpoints, the enormous roof gable at the Buddhist temple of Honganji – its size emphasised by the tiny figures of the men repairing it – dwarfs Mount Fuji, seen far off in the distance. In the middle distance, the high scaffolding of a fire-tower and a kite flying over the rooftops below can be seen. The way that the gable in the foreground is echoed in the cone of the mountain in the background is one of Hokusai's favourite compositional devices.

FUJI FROM KANAYA ON THE TOKAIDO ROAD (TOKAIDO KANAYA NO FUJI)
Series: 'Thirty-Six Views of Mount Fuji' (Fugaku sanjurokkei)
Signature: zen Hokusai Iitsu hitsu
Date: mid-1830s
CBL J 2742

Kanaya was the twenty-fourth station on the Tokaido Road, the main road between Edo and Kyoto. It was located on the Oi River and, because there was no bridge or ferry there, 'river-waders' were used to carry travellers across its swift-flowing waters. This design belongs to a group of ten additional prints to the 'Thirty-Six Views of Mount Fuji', produced in response to the phenomenal success of the original series.

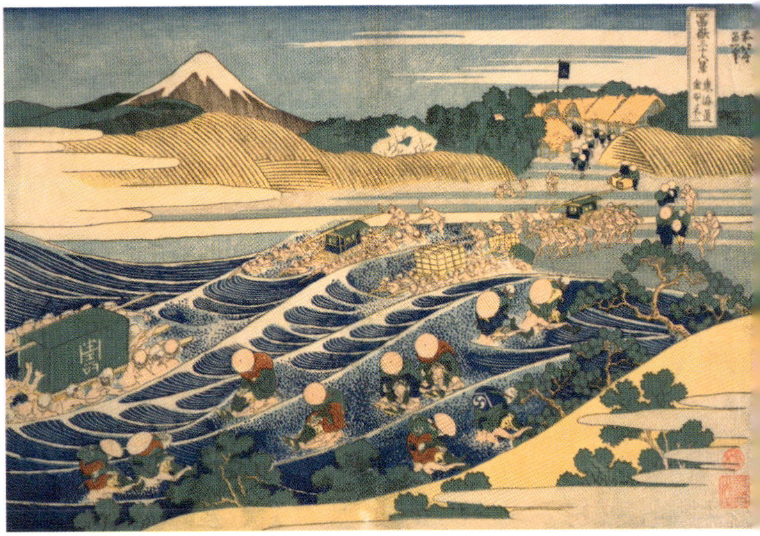

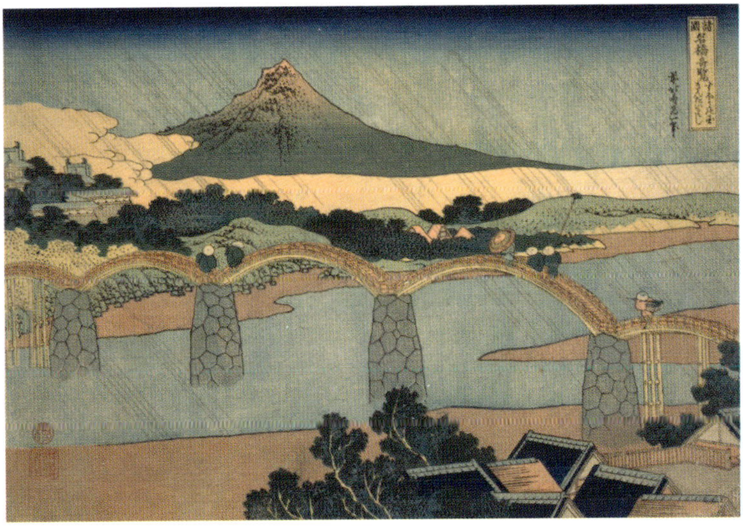

THE BRIDGE OF THE BROCADE SASH IN SUO PROVINCE (SUO NO KUNI KINTAIBASHI)
Series: 'Remarkable Views of Famous Bridges in the Provinces' (Shokoku meikyo kiran)
Signature: zen Hokusai Iitsu hitsu
Date: 1827–30
CBL J 2753

This series shows eleven bridges of different shapes and sizes. The Bridge of the Brocade Sash is named for its unusual design, consisting of five joined wooden arches raised on stone piers high above the river. A blue-robed *samurai* holds an umbrella against the rain as he crosses the bridge, but the figures on the left ignore the downpour as they pause to admire the view.

CATCHING A WHALE OFF THE GOTO ISLANDS (GOTO KUJIRA TSUKI)
Series: 'Ocean of a Thousand Pictures' (Chie no umi)
Signature: zen Hokusai Iitsu hitsu
Date: c.1833
CBL J 2771

This rare print depicts a historical event, when a whale was stranded on a sandbank off the coast of the Goto Islands in western Japan. Hokusai has drawn the whale with a walrus-like beard, huge slit eyes and spiky projections along the spine. Hokusai conveys the vast size of the whale by setting it within a ring of tiny ships.

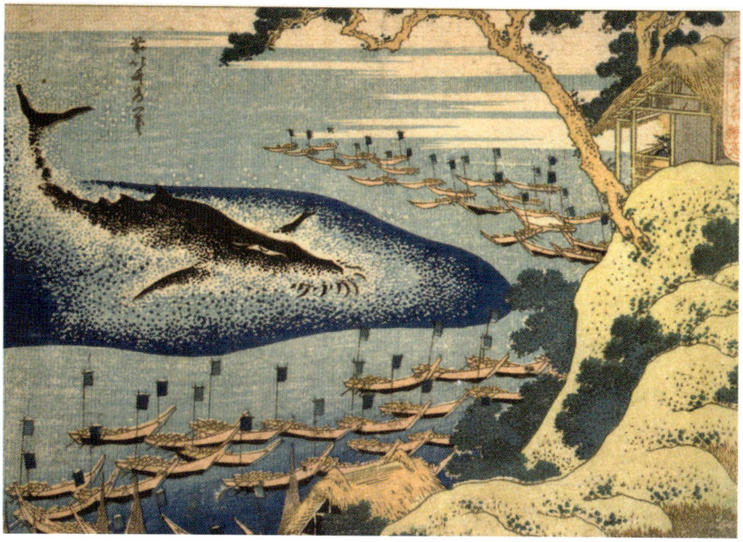

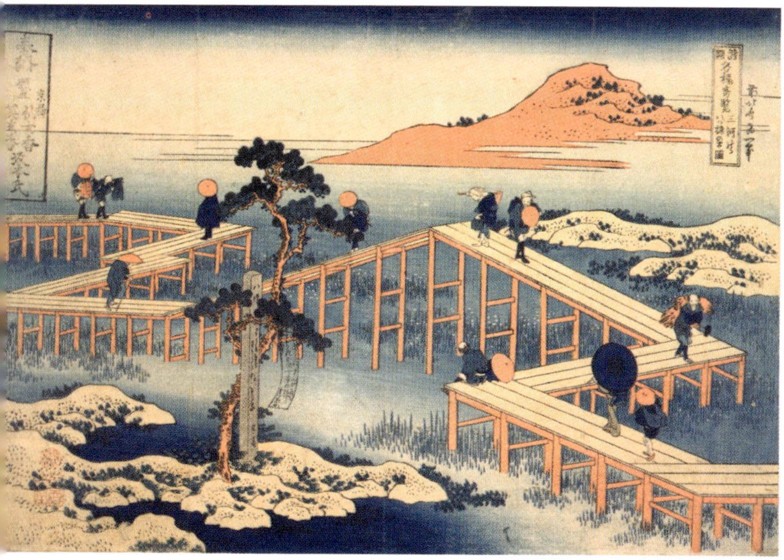

ANCIENT VIEW OF YATSUHASHI BRIDGE IN MIKAWA PROVINCE (MIKAWA YATSUHASHI NO KOZUI)
Series: 'Remarkable Views of Famous Bridges in the Provinces' (Shokoku meikyo kiran)
Signature: zen Hokusai Iitsu hitsu
Date: 1827–30
CBL J 2757

Farmers and travellers at the Yatsuhashi Bridge are admiring the irises flowering below them. Yatsuhashi literally means 'eight bridges', and it was built to span a confluence of eight different rivers. The spot was made famous through its description in the 10th-century collection of verse and prose, *The Tales of Ise*, and the motifs of the zigzag bridge and irises has been a popular one in Japanese art ever since

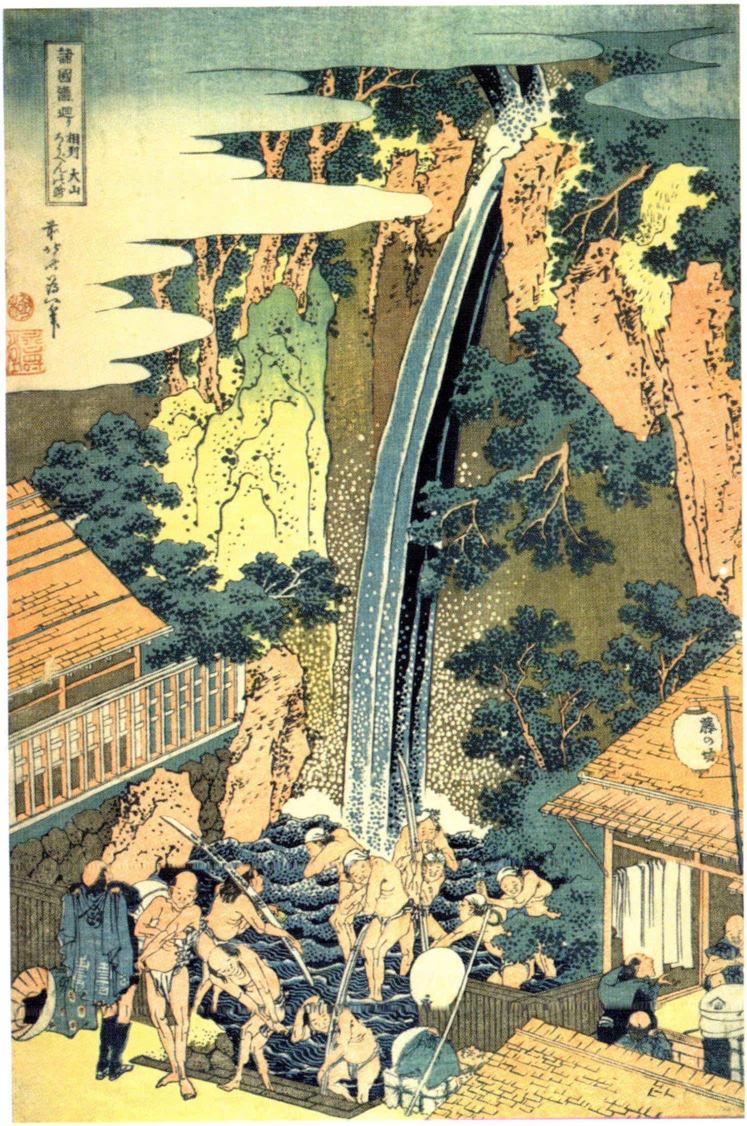

THE ROBEN WATERFALL AT OYAMA IN SAGAMI PROVINCE (SOSHU OYAMA ROBEN NO TAKI)
Series: *'Going round the Waterfalls in the Various Provinces' (Shokoku taki meguri)*
Signature: zen Hokusai Iitsu hitsu
Date: c.1832
CBL J 2761

Pilgrims take a ritual bath at the Roben Waterfall on Oyama Mountain before visiting a nearby shrine. While most of the bathers busy themselves in the water, a single pilgrim, standing beside the pool, gazes in awe at the falls. In this series, Hokusai tackled the technical problems of how to represent falling water, treating it in a different way in each of the eight prints.

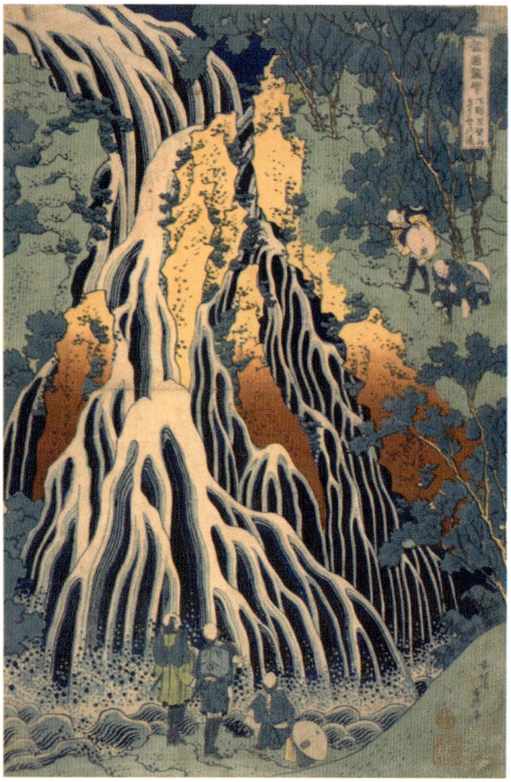

ONO WATERFALL ON THE KISOKAIDO ROAD (KISOKAIDO ONO NO BAKUFU)
Series: *'Going round the Waterfalls in the Various Provinces' (Shokoku taki meguri)*
Signature: zen Hokusai Iitsu hitsu
Date: c. 1832
CBL J 2759

A group of travellers gaze up at the Ono Waterfall. Beyond, mist rises from the mountain pass. The steep cliff to the right and the small wooden shrine perched on the crag jutting out over the pool at the base of the falls, as well as the upright format Hokusai has chosen for this series, all serve to magnify the sense of the waterfall's height (in reality less than 10 metres high).

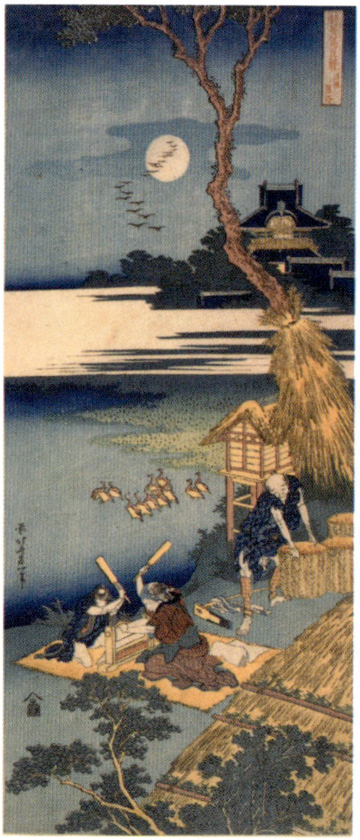

THE POET ARIWARA NO NARIHIRA
Series: 'A True Mirror of Chinese and Japanese Poets' (Shiika shashinkyo)
Signature: zen Hokusai Iitsu hitsu
Date: c. 1833
CBL J 2802

This image, from Hokusai's rare series of ten large prints illustrating works by famous classical poets, alludes to a poem by the 9th-century poet, Ariwara no Narihira, and evokes the gentle melancholy of an autumn evening. The images of a full moon, maple leaves, homing geese and the sound of cloth being beaten on a fulling block are all associated in Japanese literature with the arrival of autumn.

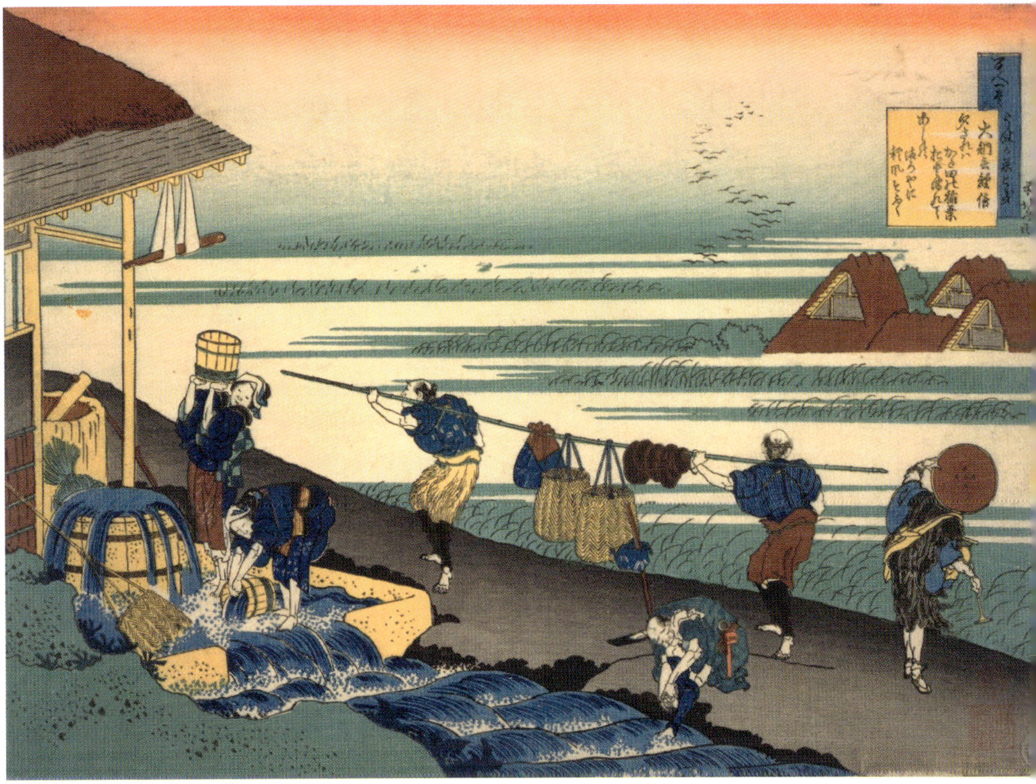

ILLUSTRATION OF THE POEM BY DAINAGON TSUNENOBU (DAINAGON TSUNENOBU)
Series: 'One Hundred Poems as explained by the Wet Nurse' (Hyakunin isshu uba ga etoki)
Signature: zen Hokusai Manji
Date: 1835–36
CBL J 2774

When evening comes
Rustling in rice leaves,
Cool autumn winds blow
Over the reed hut.

Hokusai's last series of single prints interprets this famous classical anthology of poems through the eyes of a lower-class wet nurse, as though explaining the poems to a small child. Here Hokusai illustrates the poem's image of a breezy autumn evening. A travelling monk, on the right, grasps his hat and wind bends the rice in the paddy fields in the background. The flight of geese is also symbolic of autumn. The rich colouring of this print is typical of the series.

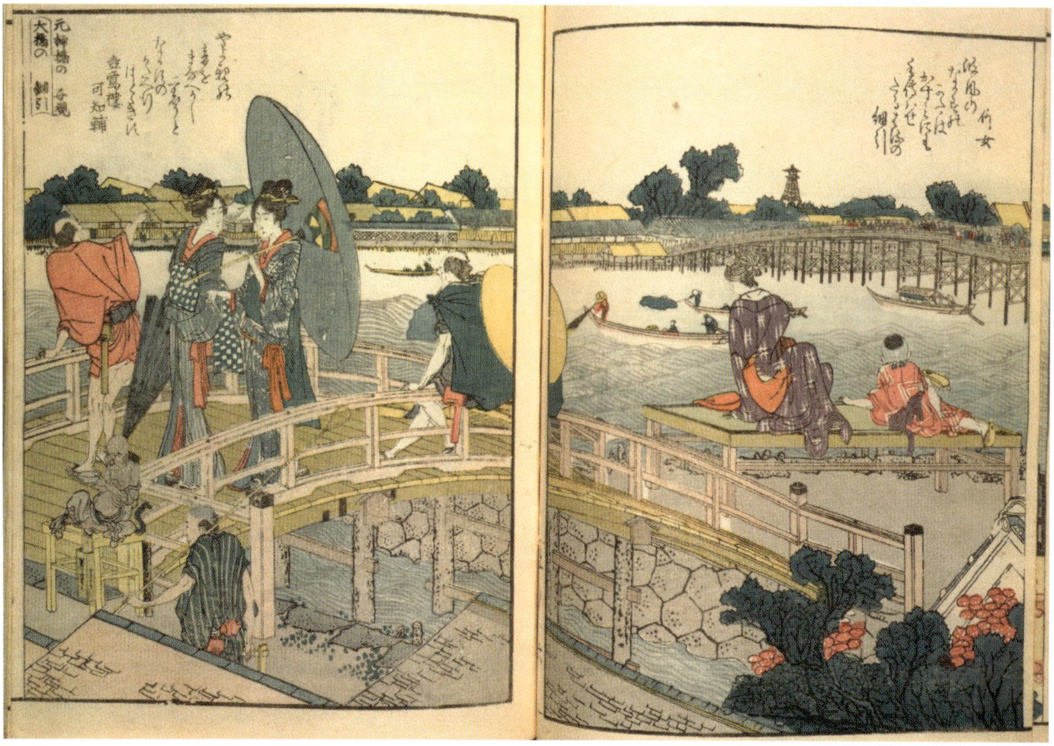

A SUMMER'S DAY BESIDE THE SUMIDA RIVER

From Both banks of the Sumida River, *vol. 1* (Ehon Sumidagawa ryogan ichiran)
Date: c. 1805
CBL J 1673

This book gives a continuous panoramic view along the banks of the Sumida River, running from one opening to the next, from right to left (Japanese books are traditionally read from right to left). With its fine use of colour and its imaginative changes of viewpoint along the river, it is considered to be one of the outstanding Japanese colour-printed books.

Each opening of the book follows the lines of the riverbank to give a continuous view, and Hokusai uses variations in seasons and weather conditions to striking pictorial effect. A close look at the openings illustrated on these pages shows that the scenes above, of men, women and children relaxing by the river in summertime, are a direct continuation of the scenes opposite, which are set several months earlier, at the height of the cherry-blossom season.

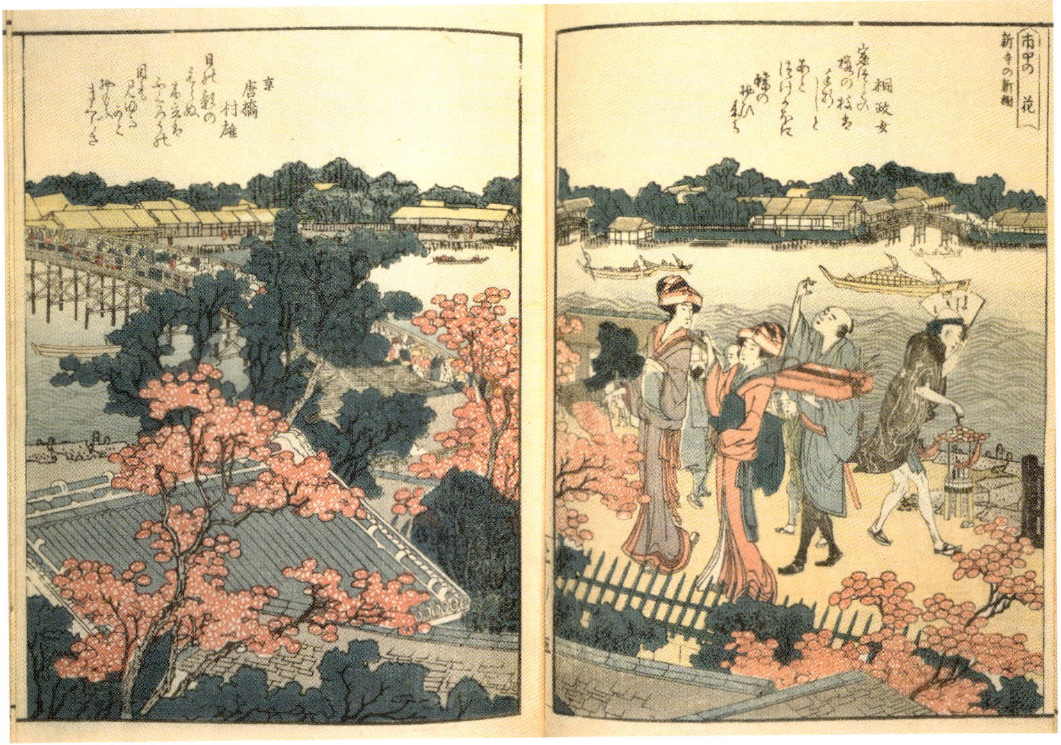

VIEWING THE CHERRY BLOSSOMS BY THE SUMIDA RIVER

From Both banks of the Sumida River, *vol. 1* (Ehon Sumidagawa ryogan ichiran)
Date: c. 1805
CBL J 1673

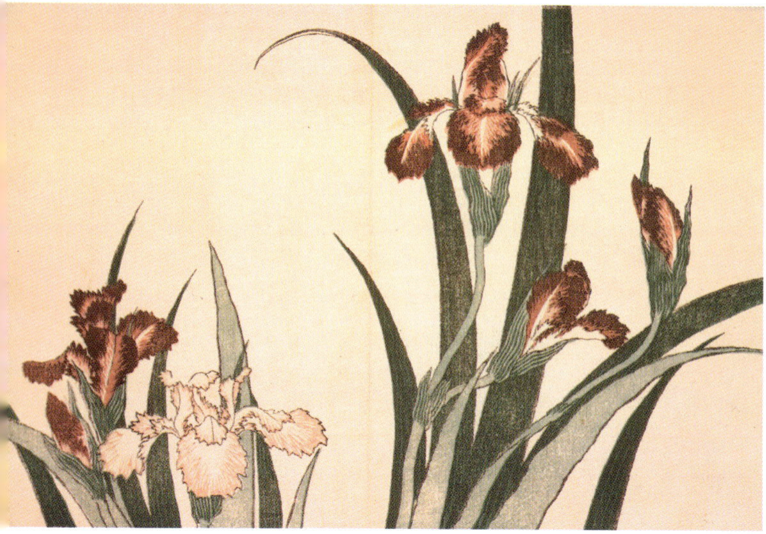

IRISES
From Hokusai's Album of Pictures from Nature (Hokusai shashin gafu)
Date: c. 1814
Japan
CBL J 1669

This album, which reworks traditional Japanese painting themes in the colour-print medium, was Hokusai's first work to go beyond the simple illustration of novels or poems, and it helped to establish his reputation as a great woodblock print designer. Its fifteen images cover a wide range of subjects, from naturalistically depicted plants and animals to landscapes, religious images and human figures.

PHEASANT
From Hokusai's Album of Pictures from Nature (Hokusai shashin gafu)
Date: c. 1814
Japan
CBL J 1669

Made with high-quality paper and printed in delicate colours, this album seems to have been privately commissioned. Perhaps because of this, relatively small numbers of copies of the work survive. Here, the strong diagonal line of the pheasant's body bisecting the space and the almost abstract depiction of the footprints against a plain background present a striking image.

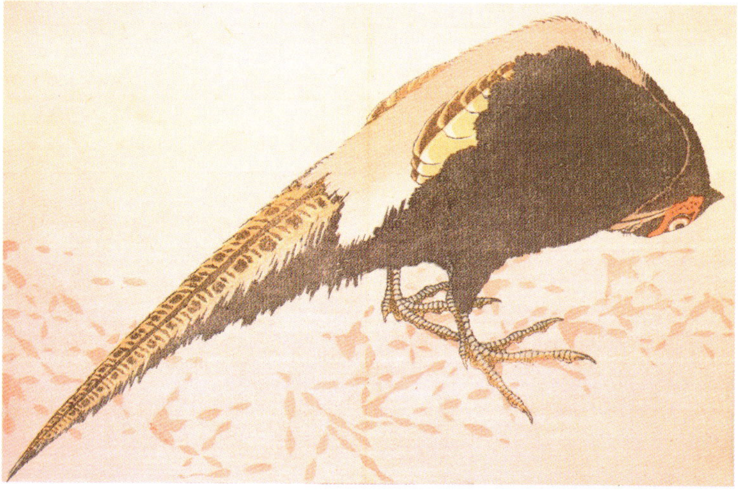

MOUNT FUJI THROUGH A BAMBOO GROVE (CHIKURIN NO FUJI)

From One Hundred Views of Mount Fuji, *vol. 2*
(Fugaku hyakkei)
Date: 1835
CBL J 1614

In this print, Mount Fuji is seen through a screen of bamboo trees. the curving stems of the trees on the right echo the silhouette of the mountain in the background.

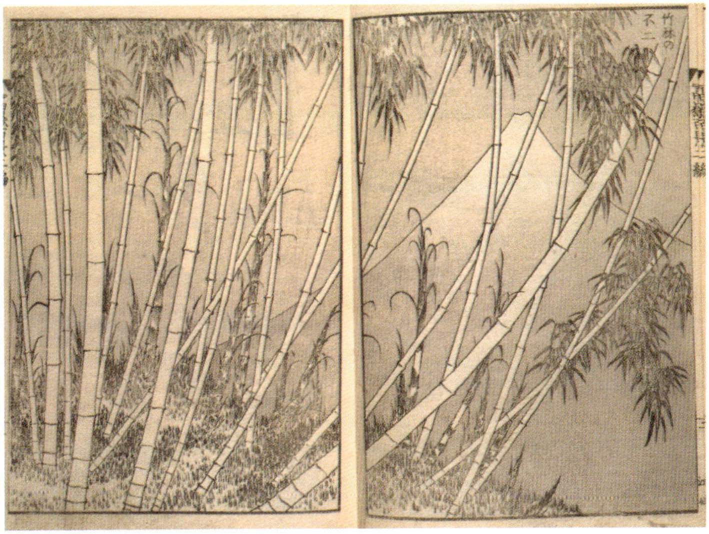

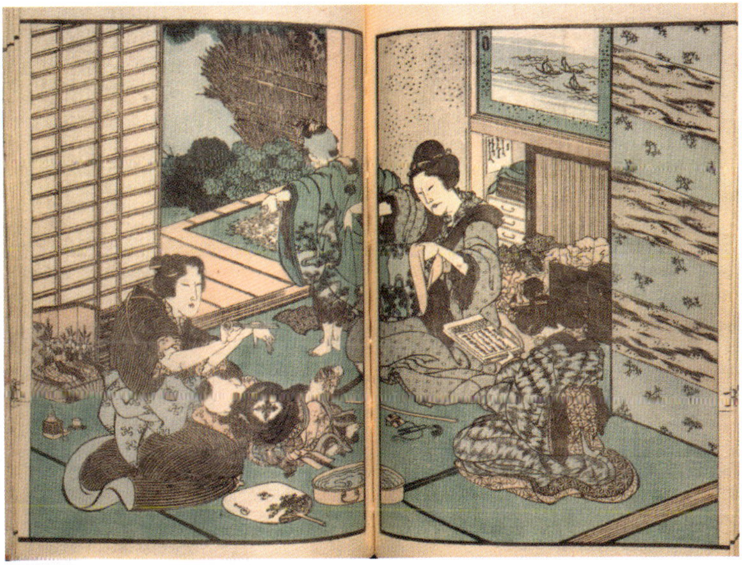

DOMESTIC INTERIOR

From The Illustrated Version of Imagawa's Teachings for Women (Ehon onna Imagawa)
Date: 1830–47
CBL J 1651

The original *Onna Imagawa*, written by a woman named Sawada Kichi in 1700, was a series of admonitions to young girls, for whom it became a standard schoolbook and a practice piece for their calligraphic exercises. Hokusai illustrates the text with an imaginative series of pictures of women exemplifying the virtues commended in the book, such as heroism, religious dedication, loyalty or domestic contentment.

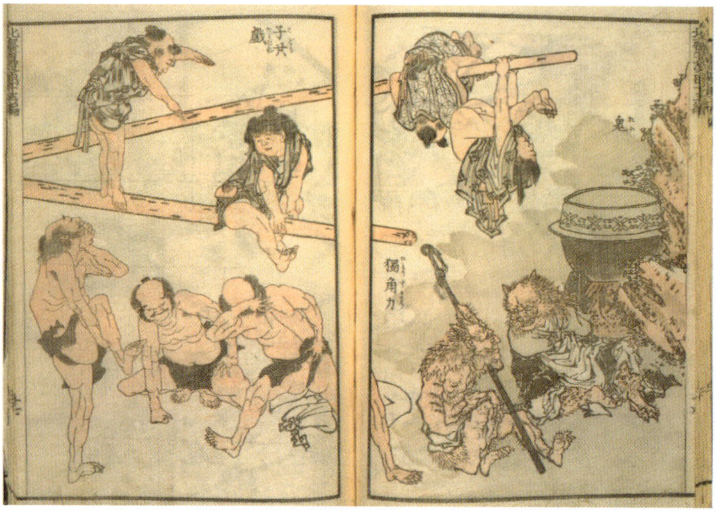

CHILDREN, DEMONS AND WRESTLERS
From Hokusai Sketches, *vol. 15* (Hokusai Manga)
Date: 1878
CBL J 1603.1

By the 1850s, copies of the *Manga* began to circulate in the West, where they were known as the *Hokusai Sketches*. As a lively, shorthand account of the exotic-seeming country that had only recently been opened to the world, the work evoked endless fascination and it played an important role in the beginning of 'Japonisme'.

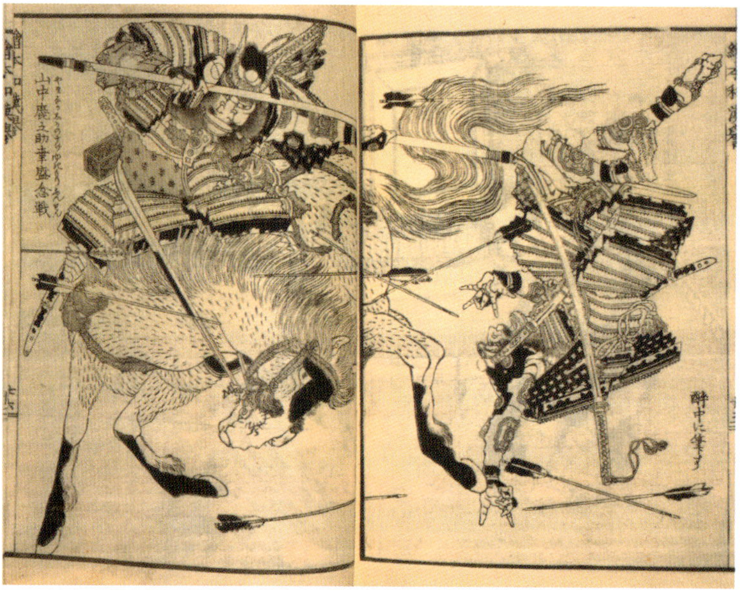

THE WARRIOR YAMANAKA CHUNOSUKE ON HORSEBACK SLAYS HIS ENEMY
From A Picture Book of the Glories of China and Japan (Ehon wakan no homare)
Date: 1850
Japan
CBL J 1615

In his final years, Hokusai produced several books of warrior prints, and this volume contains dramatic black-and-white illustrations of historical heroes of China and Japan. Printed the year after his death, its elaborate style reflects the contemporary taste for violence and bravado.

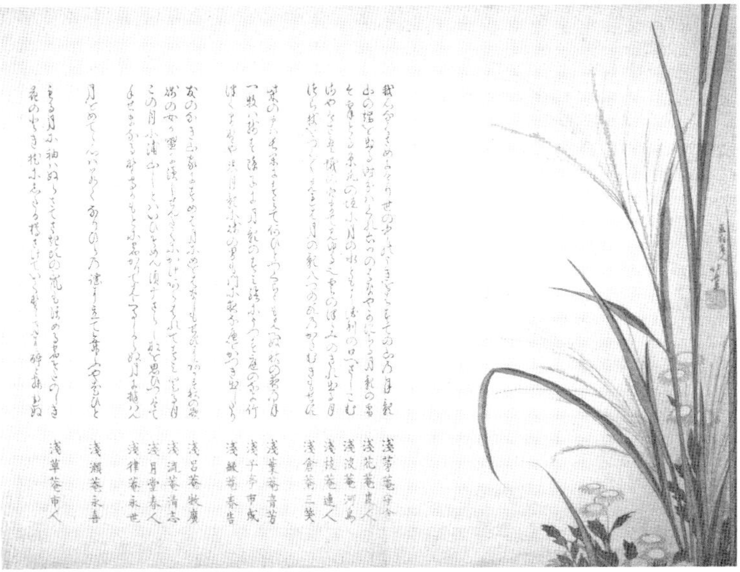

ASTERS AND PAMPAS GRASS
Signature: Gakyorojin Hokusai ga
Date: c.1805
CBL J 2820

The light of the moon is the subject of all the verses on this *surimono*, and Hokusai's flowers and grasses are printed in pale colours, as though seen by moonlight. The poems were probably composed during a moon-viewing gathering during the autumn. The poets are all members of the Asakusa poetry group.

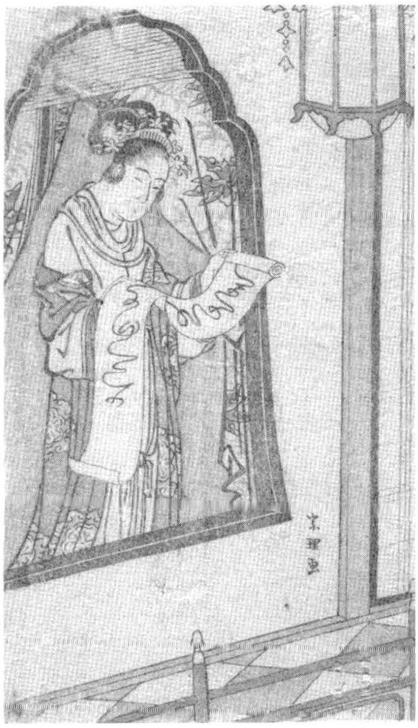

CHINESE PRINCESS STANDING AT A WINDOW
Signature: Sori ga
Date: 1796
CBL J 2154

This is a picture calendar, or *egoyomi*, with the numerals for the long months of 1796 written in cursive script on the letter in the woman's hands. The colour and design are particularly fine for an early calendar print, but there seems to be no obvious allusion to any particular legend or tale.

is a light-hearted and witty version of the traditional thirty-one-syllable Japanese poetic form of *waka*. To commemorate a particular poetry gathering, especially at the New Year, they often had their poems printed in poetry albums or on single-sheet prints and commissioned artists to illustrate them. Unlike the commercially printed *ukiyo-e*, these *surimono* were distributed as gifts to a limited circle of friends – in the same way that we send Christmas cards today.

Because money was no object, *surimono* were usually made in small numbers (around 75–100 impressions, as opposed to several hundred or even thousands in the case of popular commercial prints), using top-quality materials and elaborate printing techniques. *Surimono* designers, therefore, had considerable freedom to experiment with the effects of detailed engraving of fine lines, subtle shading, wide ranges of colours (including expensive gold, silver and copper dust) and blind-printing – a method of embossing made possible by the thickness of the high-quality paper used.

With both albums and single-sheet *surimono*, the themes of the pictures were provided by the poems that appeared in them, or by the specific requirements of the patron who commissioned a print for a special occasion. The artist's skill lay in how he chose to illustrate the given themes. Hokusai, who seems to have moved in the circles of these urban literati after leaving the Katsukawa School, demonstrated great skill and sensitivity in his illustrations of poetic themes. His delicately coloured, elegant works – radically different in style from his earlier actor portraits and often set in the countryside in and around Edo – were in great demand by the end of the 18th century.

Hokusai's earliest *surimono* were a number of illustrated calendar prints, or 'picture calendars' *(egoyomi)*, designed in 1789. In the lunar calendar, used in Japan until the late-19th century, a year was composed of alternating long and short months. These varied from year to year and, at the beginning of each year, the government announced which months would be long (thirty days) and which would be short (twenty-nine days). It was forbidden for anyone but the government to issue a calendar giving this information, but calendars were popular New Year's gifts and print designers got round the prohibition by producing prints with the numbers of the months hidden in the illustrations.

Hokusai went on to design hundreds of single-sheet *surimono* during the early years of the 19th century, some announcing special events and some commemorating poetry gatherings, and many for the New Year. He also contributed to numerous *kyoka* poetry albums, which were usually collaborative ventures employing the talents of a number of different artists. Hokusai continued to produce *surimono* throughout his career, although, by the 1810s, his focus had begun to shift towards the landscapes for which he is now most famous.

Landscape Prints

Both in Japan and the West, Hokusai's reputation is based, above all, on the landscape designs he produced in the 1820s and 1830s, when he was in his sixties and seventies.

The landscape had long been an important category of East Asian art. As early as the 5th century, scholar-painters in China had established the landscape as a subject for expressing philosophical principles as well as for interpreting natural beauty. In Japan, idealised landscapes in the Chinese tradition, which attempted to portray universal, spiritual themes rather than specific topographies, were considered one of the highest forms of painting. In the art of *ukiyo-e*, however, which was directed at an audience more concerned with the plebeian and sensual than the abstract and spiritual, there was at first little room for the landscape except to provide context. In most early prints, landscapes were simply used to provide a setting for figures of actors or fashionable women. In technical terms, too, the woodblock-print medium, with its stark, clear-cut outlines, was less suited to the depiction of landscape than the subtle gradations of tone used in classical ink painting.

By the early-19th century, however, conditions were ripe for the development of the landscape-print genre. By Hokusai's day, the residents of Edo, benefiting from the general economic prosperity of the times, increasingly indulged in outdoor leisure activities. To the classical, floating-world pastimes of theatres and brothels were added a whole variety of outdoor sightseeing activities – such as flower-viewing, pilgrimages to temples and shrines, festivals, boat trips along the Sumida River, and excursions to hot springs or to the coast. As this 'culture of movement' developed, so a demand arose for images of well-known landmarks in Edo and of people's activities in and around them, and the late-18th century saw the publication of growing numbers of illustrated guidebooks known as *meisho zue* ('illustrated famous places'). These early works would have provided later artists with models to consider and rework in response to publishers' demands. For in the highly competitive world of the Edo publishing industry, publishers were constantly trying to develop new markets for colour woodblock prints. Landscapes were just one of several new categories of prints that began to be marketed at around the same time, along with prints of warriors and bird-and-flower compositions.

Technical as well as commercial factors also played an important part in the emergence of the landscape-print genre. Firstly, printers discovered how to apply the pigment to give a gradation of colour on the paper. This technique, known as *bokashi,* made it possible for the first time to create subtle depictions of sky, water or scenery. Also significant was the introduction of a new Western pigment known as Prussian, or Berlin, blue. From 1829, the pigment began to be imported in sufficient quantities, and at low enough prices, to be commercially viable. Unlike earlier Japanese blues, which had been highly fugitive and unstable, the brilliantly coloured Prussian blue gave artists considerably more freedom of expression, especially in the depiction of sky and water.

Hokusai was the first print designer to take advantage of these new possibilities to establish the landscape print as an independent genre. He had begun depicting scenic locations in and around Edo in privately published *kyoka* poetry albums at the end of the 18th century, but his first series of 'pure' landscapes was produced in the early 1800s, in response to Western painting. With his insatiable appetite for artistic learning, Hokusai had, by now, not only studied various schools of traditional Japanese and Chinese painting, but had turned to Western painting for inspiration. Western art had first really made its presence felt in Japan in the late-16th century, but its influence was curtailed when the *shoguns*, fearing for national security, closed Japan to foreigners in 1639 and maintained a strict isolation policy for

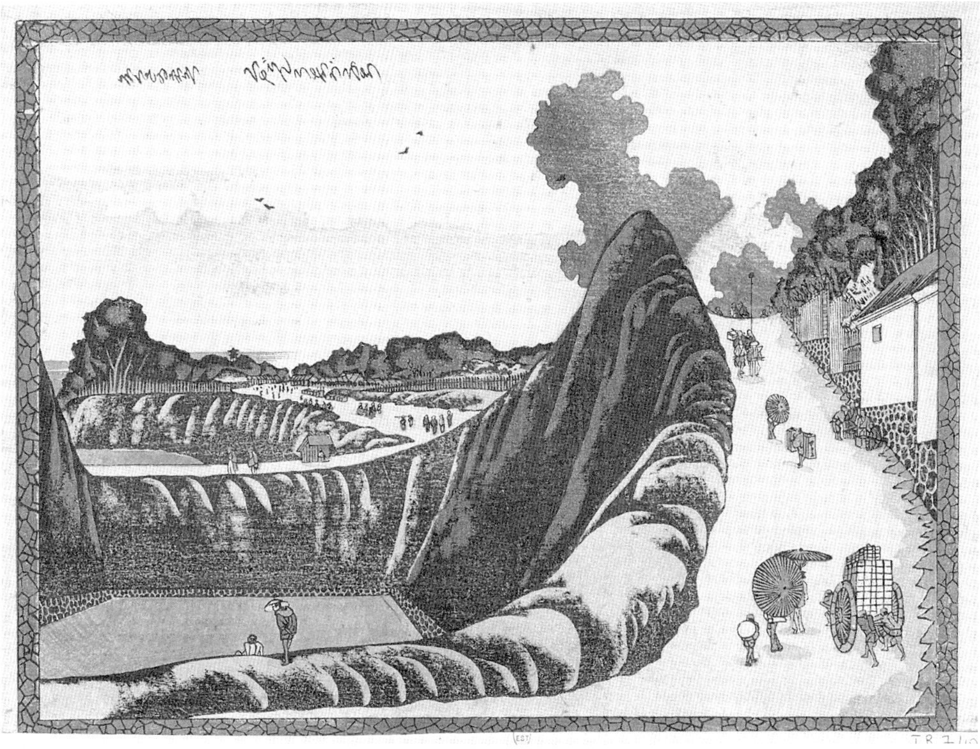

USHIGAFUCHI AT KUDAN (KUDAN USHIGAFUCHI)
From a group of Western-style landscapes
Signed: Hokusai gaku
Date: c.1800–05
Bibliothèque nationale de France, Paris (JB. 740)

It is a sunny day and, on the right people are walking up Ushigafuchi Street. On the left, two men gaze down into Ushigafuchi Pool, which gave the area its name. A strong Western influence can be seen in the cast shadows, *chiaroscuro* shading and realistically depicted clouds of the print. Hokusai has further emphasised the Western feel of the picture by adding a frame-like border and by writing his signature and the title of the print in horizontal, syllabic script.

the next two centuries. During this period of isolation, however, trade was maintained on a modest scale with the Chinese and Dutch and, through this strictly controlled contact, some knowledge of the outside world reached Japan. By the last decades of the 18th century, a number of illustrated Dutch books and prints had been imported and knowledge of copperplate engraving, oil painting and other techniques was diffused.

The realism of European art, in particular, fascinated Japanese artists and, between 1800 and 1805, Hokusai published a set of prints experimenting with Western artistic conventions, such as linear perspective and *chiaroscuro* shading to indicate depth, light and shadow, complete with decorative borders in imitation of the frames around oil paintings and with titles written horizontally in Western style. Hokusai continued to experiment with landscapes for a while, producing single prints of traditional views of Edo and of scenes along the Tokaido Road that linked Edo with Kyoto. He also depicted landscapes in a number of his illustrated books. However, it was not until the late-1820s that he produced the series of prints that are considered his masterpieces of landscape design.

Hokusai's most acclaimed landscape series was the 'Thirty-Six Views of Mount Fuji', produced from the end of the 1820s with the publisher Nishimuraya Yohachi. The series depicted Japan's sacred mountain from different viewpoints, under different climatic conditions, during different seasons and at different times of day, and was so popular that an extra ten prints were commissioned (bringing the total number of views to forty-six, rather than the thirty-six of the series title). Several reprints of the series were issued, and a number of contemporary artists were inspired by its example, including Japan's other great designer of landscape prints, Ando Hiroshige (1797–1858).

The success of the series was largely due to its novelty, both in terms of subject matter and of style. It was the first ever series of large-scale, single-sheet landscape prints in the history of Japanese printmaking. Although many of the images showed humans interacting with nature, the landscape was invariably given as much, if not more, weight within the composition.
The focus on the theme of Mount Fuji also contributed to its popularity, for

the beautiful mountain, which had always been a favourite subject for poets and painters, was enjoying a period of particular veneration in Edo at the time. The sacred mountain was a popular pilgrimage site and miniature versions were built all over the city for those unable to climb the real peak. With its simple, yet well-chosen, colour schemes and bold compositions, the series was also stylistically ground-breaking, combining elements of Japanese, Chinese and Western painting into a unique individual style. Unlike Hokusai's earlier landscape prints, with their often exaggerated Western style, the 'Thirty-Six Views' found a balance between Japanese traditional and Western influences. Ironically, it was his effective incorporation of European traditions into his work that was to win him swifter appreciation in the West than any other *ukiyo-e* artist and that first helped Western artists to liberate themselves from those same traditions.

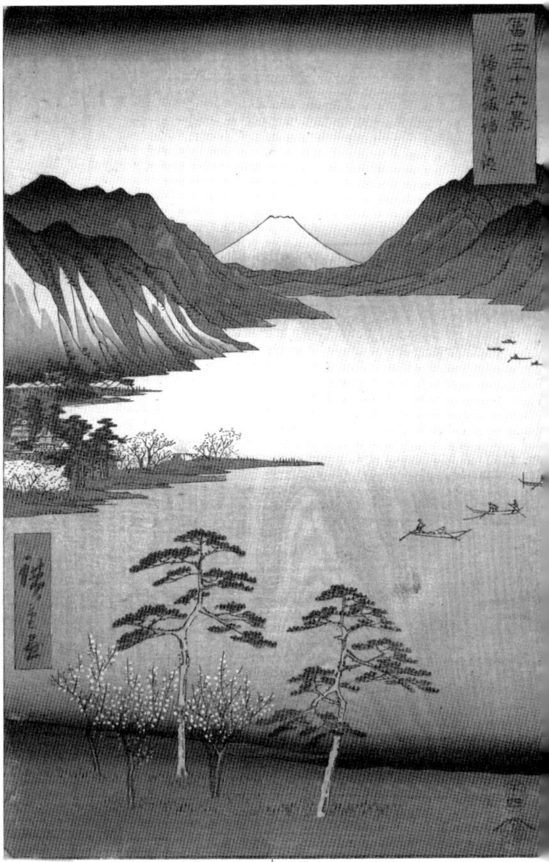

SUWA LAKE IN SHINANO PROVINCE
(SHINSHU SUWANOKO)
Series: 'Thirty-Six Views of Mount Fuji' (Fuji sanjurokkei)
By: Ando Hiroshige
Signed: Hiroshige ga
Date: 1858
CBL J 2714

Mount Fuji can be seen in the background of this peaceful view of Lake Suwa in the springtime. Hiroshige's series of prints of Mount Fuji was probably inspired by the phenomenal success of Hokusai's series of the 1830s.

While he was working on the 'Thirty-Six Views', Hokusai published several other major landscape series, including views of waterfalls, bridges and scenes of the Ryukyu Islands, a semi-autonomous archipelago to the south of Japan. At the same time as these notable landscape prints were being published, he also designed two striking sets of images of flowers and birds. However, none was as successful as the 'Thirty-Six Views' and all were printed in relatively small editions. The limited demand may have been partly due to a serious economic recession in the mid-1830s, which badly affected print and book production. Hokusai, like many other artists, suffered from the economic problems, and it is reported that, during the worst of this crisis, he wandered through the streets of Edo trying to sell his drawings. Even after the crisis was over, Hokusai – by now in his early eighties – never returned to his former level of production. He withdrew gradually from the field of colour prints and devoted more and more of his time to illustrated books and brush paintings until his death in his ninetieth year.

Illustrated Books

In Hokusai's day, an artist's reputation was established as much by his contributions to printed books as by his paintings, or even his single-sheet prints. This was because there were no exhibition galleries to bring paintings to the attention of the general public, while there were huge numbers of booksellers and lending libraries. Single-sheet prints were sold at bookstalls too, but were never as widely circulated as books.

Although nowadays we know him best for his individual prints, Hokusai also illustrated some 270 printed books, published between 1780, when he was just twenty, and 1849, the year of his death. He began with monochrome illustrations of works of cheap popular novels known as *kibyoshi* (literally 'yellowbacks'), some of which he wrote himself. By the 1790s, he was producing privately published, luxury editions of illustrated *kyoka* poetry anthologies and, by the turn of the century, he was devoting much of his energy to illustrating full-length fiction works known as *yomihon* (literally 'reading books'). These works, based on Chinese and Japanese classics of historical fiction and sometimes extending to as many as a hundred volumes, were hugely popular at the time, and Hokusai's dramatic designs won him great public acclaim. He also produced a number of albums of erotic prints as well as pattern books for craftsmen, providing designs for items such as combs, pipe stems and dyed fabrics. In the 1810s, however, he turned his attention to the production of art manuals *(etehon)*, containing model sketches primarily for use by his pupils and followers.

The most successful of these manuals was undoubtedly the *Hokusai Manga*, the first volume of which was published in 1814. The term *manga* literally means 'random' or 'miscellaneous' sketches. The work seems to have come about after a visit to the town of Nagoya, when a group of admirers enrolled themselves as his pupils and persuaded him to have a number of model sketches published as a kind of textbook of instruction on drawing in the Hokusai style. The book, a series of hundreds of disconnected drawings of lively figures from everyday life, history and legend, immediately achieved enormous popularity, not just with art students, but with the public at large. Ten volumes of the *Manga* were published over the next five years and five further volumes appeared later at irregular intervals, including two volumes published posthumously. In total, the *Manga* included nearly 4,000 designs, illustrating a comprehensive range of subjects including animals, birds, insects, flowers, fish and landscapes as well as human figures. So successful were the *Manga* that they were still being reprinted as late as the 1870s – although, by then, the blocks had become severely worn.

Phenomenally popular in Japan, the *Manga* were also widely acclaimed in the West, where they were known as the *Hokusai Sketches*. Images from the work had already reached Europe during Hokusai's lifetime, in the form of lithographed versions used to illustrate an account of Japan published in 1831 by the resident physician to the Dutch trading post, Philipp Franz von Siebold. By the 1850s, actual copies of the *Manga* began to circulate among French artists and played an important role in the beginning of the enthusiasm for things Japanese that became known as 'Japonisme'. Indeed, it is said to have been a copy of Hokusai's *Manga*, discovered as packing material in a crate of imported ceramics by the French etcher Félix Bracquemond in the mid-1850s, that first sparked the Japan craze. Not only were the volumes more accessible than most Japanese books, because so many had been published over the years, but they also evoked endless fascination as a lively, shorthand account of the exotic-seeming country that had only recently been opened to the world after centuries of seclusion. Designs taken from the *Manga* volumes began to figure in all kinds of publications, and also in the graphic and decorative arts.

Also hugely successful, both in Japan and the West, was the book generally considered to be Hokusai's greatest masterpiece of book illustration, the *One Hundred Views of Mount Fuji (Fugaku hyakkei)*. Following the tremendous success of the 'Thirty-Six Views' series, the *One Hundred Views* was an expansion in book form of the variations he had tried in single-sheet format.

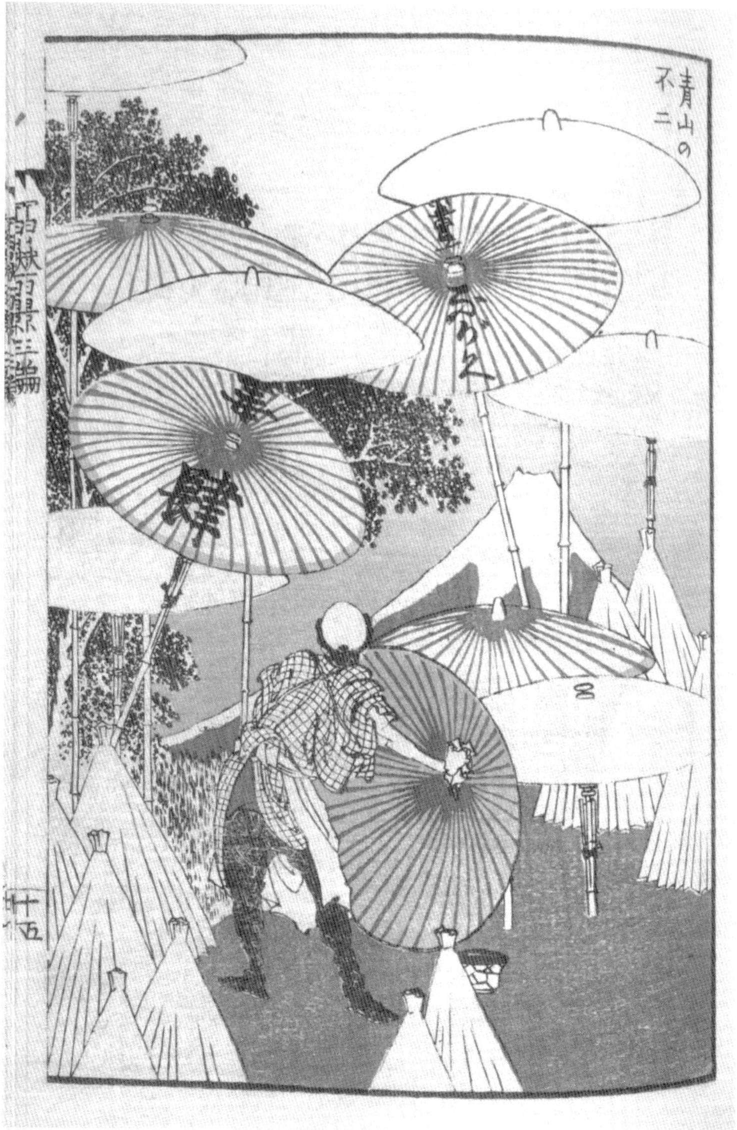

FUJI SEEN FROM AN UMBRELLA-MAKER'S YARD IN AOYAMA (AOYAMA NO FUJI)
From One Hundred Views of Mount Fuji, *vol. 2*
(Fugaku hyakkei)
Date: 1835
CBL J 1614

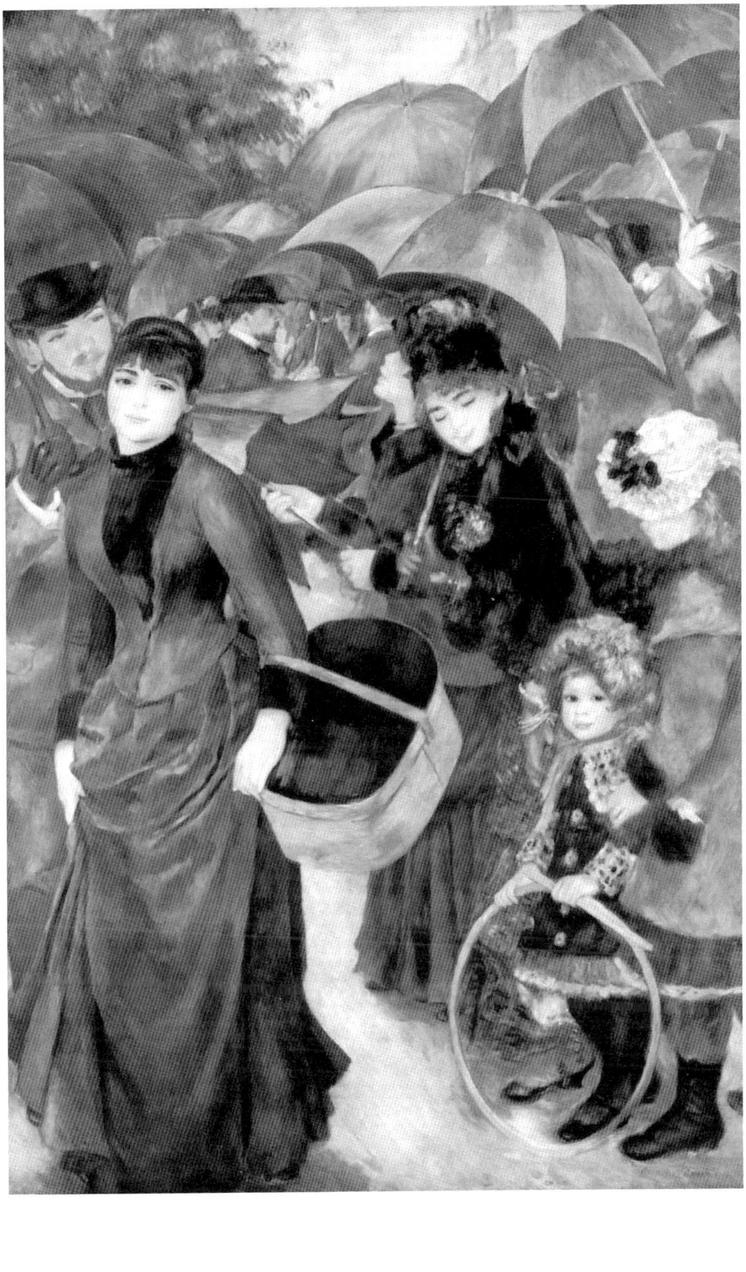

LES PARAPLUIES
By Pierre-Auguste Renoir
Medium: Oil on canvas
Date: c. 1881–6
National Gallery, London

ASSORTED BIRDS
From Hokusai Sketches,
vol. 15 (Hokusai Manga)
Date: 1878
CBL J 1603.1

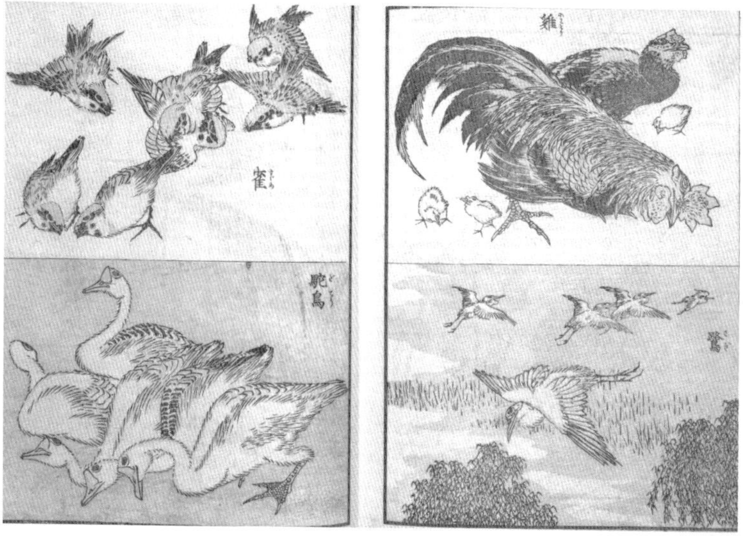

STONEWARE PLATE WITH MANGA-INSPIRED DESIGN OF COCKEREL
Designed by: Félix Bracquemond and Eugène Rousseau
Date: 1866
Victoria & Albert Museum

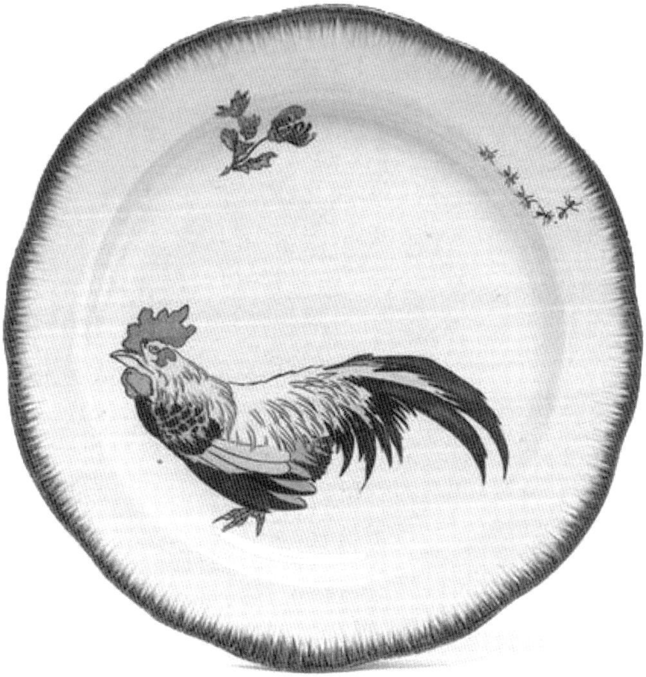

By 1834, when the first volume of the *One Hundred Views* was published, Hokusai was at the height of his powers, and the work, with its skilled draughtsmanship and inventive compositions, epitomises his artistic philosophy and practice. Two further volumes were published, one in 1835 and one in 1849, the year of his death. Although the work was produced in monochrome, the first edition of each volume was carved by the foremost block-cutters of the time in such exquisite detail that the subtle gradations of grey and black ink give the effect of a range of colours. Like the *Manga*, the *One Hundred Views of Mount Fuji* became well known to European artists, illustrators and graphic designers, who took inspiration from Hokusai's genius for composition and from his use of a variety of viewpoints, angles and moods.

Epilogue

It is an interesting fact that Hokusai's art exerted more influence on Western art than on Japanese art, even though he had a large number of students, both official and unofficial. He had been teaching young artists since the late 1790s and we know of as many as two hundred Hokusai pupils, many of whom expressed their allegiance by taking an art name related to his, such as Hokkei or Hokuba. Nevertheless, it is not possible to speak of a Hokusai School, largely because he changed his own style so often that work by his followers varies considerably. None of his pupils was particularly outstanding and, as a result, he did not make a lasting impression on the art of Japan.

In Europe and America, however, Hokusai became widely known at a time when artistic traditions were in a state of flux and avant-garde artists were desperately looking for new direction, away from the realism of academic painting. By the end of the 19th century, even the Impressionists were feeling their limitations. As Renoir declared in the mid-1880s, "I had come to the end of Impressionism and was forced to see that I could neither paint nor draw. In a word, I was in a blind alley." A fresh form of visualisation was needed and Japanese art arrived on the scene at exactly the right time.

Although woodblock prints were considered very much a popular art in Japan, they were a revelation to Europeans and permanently altered the Western view of painting. The use of areas of flat, bright colour, the bold cropping of figures or scenes, the lack of symmetry, the absence of light and shade, the stylisation of nature and the lack of geometric perspective in the work of Japanese artists – of whom Hokusai was the most popular and widely known – represented a whole new way of looking at a picture. To Impressionist and Post-Impressionist artists from Manet to Van Gogh, Gauguin to Klimt, not to mention graphic designers, book illustrators and decorative artists such as René Lalique and Charles Comfort Tiffany, the encounter with Japanese prints spelt liberation from the traditions of European art and acted as a major force in the development of modern art.

Postscript

"I was in the habit of sketching the appearance of things about me from around the age of six. Although I had produced numerous designs by my fiftieth year, nothing I did before my seventieth year was really worth counting. Now, at the age of seventy-three, I have begun to understand the true form of birds, animals, insects and fish, and the nature of plants and trees. If I continue in this way, by the age of eighty I hope to have made even more progress and, at ninety, to have got closer to the essence of art. At the age of one hundred I will surely have reached a magnificent level and at one hundred and ten each dot and line will be alive. I would like to ask those who outlive me to observe that I have not spoken without reason."

Manji, the Old Man Mad about Painting (Gakyorojin Manji)
Postscript to Hokusai's book *One Hundred Views of Mount Fuji*

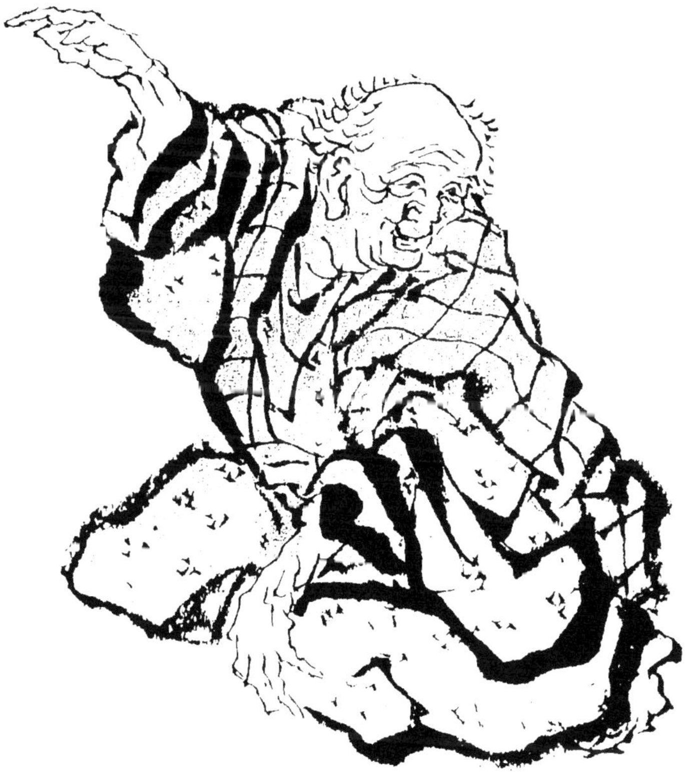

SELF-PORTRAIT OF HOKUSAI AT THE AGE OF EIGHTY-THREE
Date: 1842
National Museum of Ethnology, Leiden (3513-1496)

Further Reading

Forrer, Matthi, *Hokusai – Prints and Drawings* (Royal Academy of Arts and Prestel-Verlag, 1991).

Hillier, J, *Hokusai* (Phaidon Press, 1955).

Hillier, Jack, *The Art of Hokusai in Book Illustration* (Sotheby Parke Bernet/Philip Wilson Publishers, 1980).

Illing, Richard, *The Art of Japanese Prints* (Gallery Books, 1980).

Keyes, Roger, *The Art of Surimono – Privately published Japanese woodblock prints and books in the Chester Beatty Library, Dublin* (Sotheby/Philip Wilson Publishers, 1985).

Nagata, Seiji, *Hokusai – Genius of the Japanese Ukiyo-e* (Kodansha International, 1995).

Wichmann, Siegfried, *Japonisme – The Japanese influence on Western art since 1858* (Thames & Hudson Ltd, 1981).